THE GREAT WORLD CHALLENGE

Europe

Vinita Zutshi's fascination with words led to her becoming a writer. She enjoys writing both fiction and non-fiction for children and adults, and has created innovative formats in personalised writing. *The Great India Challenge* and *The Great World Challenge: Asia* were born from her daughter's enchantment with the social sciences—and Vinita's ignorance of it!

Find out more about Vinita's work on www.vinitazutshi.com. You can contact her at vinita@vinitazutshi.com.

To Jai—for structure, routine, ideas and help.

Roam the world knowing the adventure is in your heart.

Published by Scholastic India Pvt. Ltd.
A subsidiary of Scholastic Inc., New York, 10012 (USA).
Publishers since 1920, with international operations in Canada, Australia, New Zealand, the United Kingdom, India, and Hong Kong.

For information regarding permission, write to:
Scholastic India Pvt. Ltd.
A-27, Ground Floor, Sigma Centre
Infocity-1, Sector 34, Gurgaon-122001 (India)

First edition: August 2015
This reprint edition: November 2025

ISBN-13: 978-93-5103-995-2

Printed at Saurabh Printers Pvt.Ltd

The Great World Challenge

EUROPE

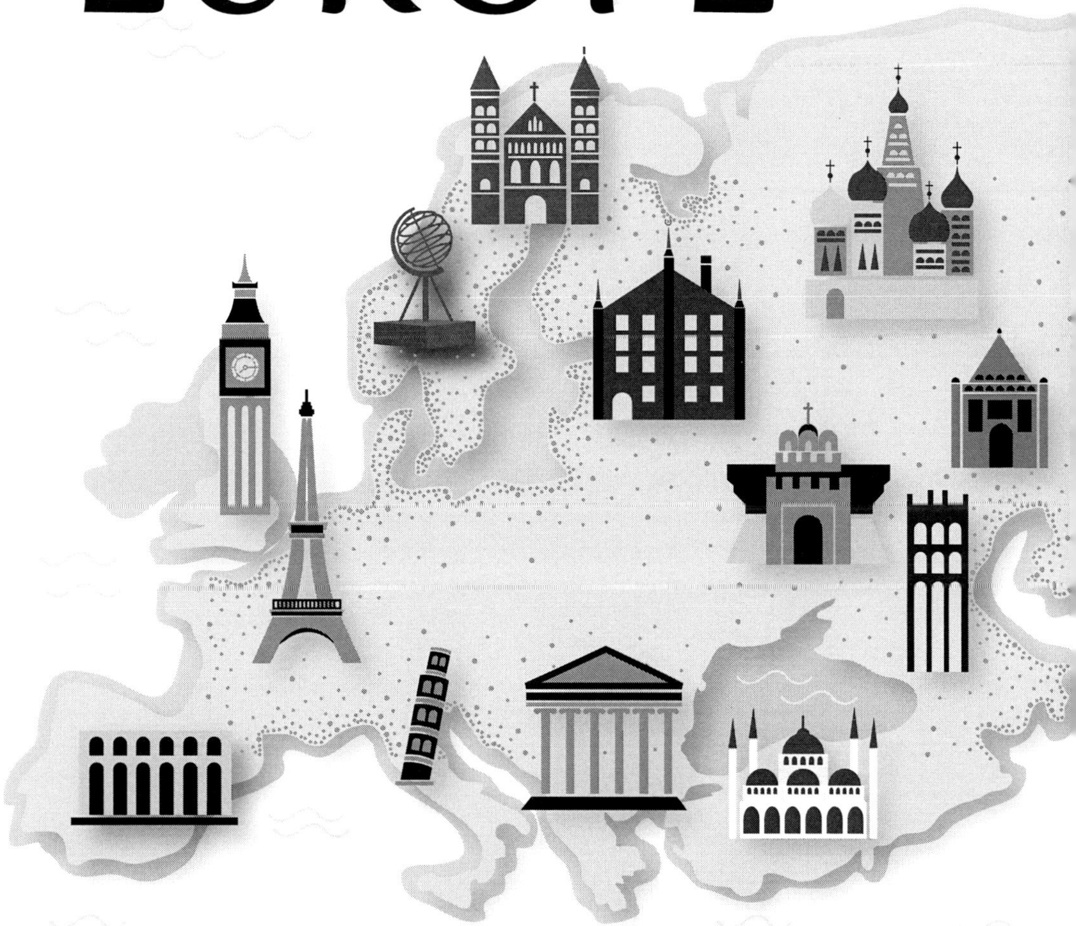

Vinita Zutshi

Illustrated & designed by Meghna Baruah

SCHOLASTIC

New York Toronto London Auckland

Sydney New Delhi Hong Kong

ACKNOWLEDGEMENTS

This book would not have been possible without the extraordinary patience and grace of the lovely Tina Narang, Publisher, Scholastic India, as I defaulted on my delivery date, again and yet again. I'll do better next time, Tina!

CONTENTS

AUTHOR'S NOTE

Landmasses are no respecter of country lines, so there is no easy way to divide Eurasia into Europe and Asia. The accepted convention for doing so is along the Bosphorus Strait, the Dardanelles Strait, and the Caucasus and Ural mountain ranges. This fails to provide a clear solution because many countries are transcontinental.

For this book, countries have been included in Europe based on population distribution within the country. So Russia is considered part of Europe, while Turkey, Kazakhstan, Azerbaijan, Georgia and Armenia have been included in Asia.

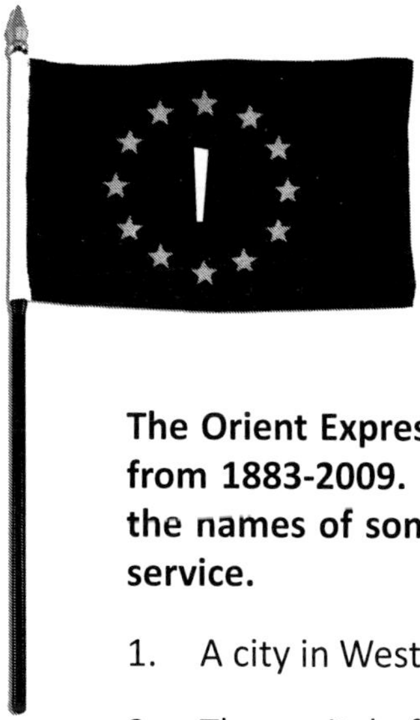

ORIENT EXPRESS

The Orient Express was a long-distance passenger service train that ran from 1883-2009. Fill one letter in each blank to solve the clue and find the names of some major cities served by the train when it first began service.

1. A city in Western Europe associated with luxury and fashion. _ _ _ _ _
2. The capital of the Alsace region in Eastern France, this city has a Germanic name because it is historically German-speaking.

   _ _ _ _ _ _ _ _ _ _ _
3. The third-largest city in Germany, its name derives from the monks of the Benedictine order who founded the city. _ _ _ _ _ _
4. This city is host to the United Nations. _ _ _ _ _ _
5. This city (and its name) was created by unifying two cities originally occupying the west and east banks of the river Danube. _ _ _ _ _ _ _ _
6. This is the largest city in Romania. _ _ _ _ _ _ _ _ _
7. The largest city in Turkey, it was part of the historic Silk Route.

   _ _ _ _ _ _ _ _

DELICIOUS SHAPES

Given below are the names of ten types of pasta. Match the shape to the correct name.

Shape of Pasta		**Name**	
1.		a.	Fusilli
2.		b.	Alfabeto
3.		c.	Ravioli
4.		d.	Penne
5.		e.	Macaroni

6.		f.	Farfalle
7.	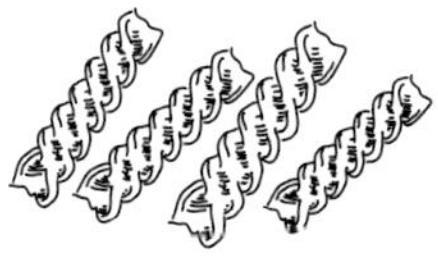	g.	Cannelloni
8.		h.	Rotelle
9.		i.	Conchiglie
10.		j.	Tagliatelle

ARTY ADDITIONS

Join two letter groups from the box below to make the surnames of famous European artists. You have two clues: some information about the artist and his/her first name.

Gre	Mi	Kli	Bens	Anne	Goya
Mo	De	Ro	Celli	Net	Net
Cez	Cha	Botti	Oir	Co	Guin
Mt	Velaz	Ru	Gas	Ren	Ee
Kl	De	Ma	Gau	Quez	Gall

1. This French painter and sculptor is known for his superb depiction of movement. More than half of his artistic works depict dancers. **Edgar** __________

2. One of the first 19th century artists to paint modern life, this French painter is credited for the beginning of modern art. He had a lifelong interest in the subject of how the elite spent their leisure time, and many of his paintings are on this subject. **Édouard** ______________

3. An Italian painter of the Early Renaissance, he belonged to the Florentine school under the patronage of Lorenzo de' Medici. **Sandro** _______________

4. Born Doménikos Theotokópoulos, this painter, sculptor and architect of the Spanish Renaissance is better known by his nickname, a reference to his national origin. He is best known for his elongated figures and fantastic pigmentation. **El** ______________

5. Known for his baroque style, this Flemish painter is one of the most famous and successful European artists of the 17th century. His works focussed on religious pictures, mythological scenes, classical and modern history and portraits. **Peter Paul** ________________

6. A Spanish court painter and printmaker, he is regarded as the last of the Old Masters and the first of the moderns. He is known for his scenes of violence, prompted by the French invasion of Spain. **Francisco de** ___________

7. This French painter's work formed the bridge between late Impressionism and early 20th century Cubism. He used planes of colour and small brushstrokes that built up to form complex fields, and was interested in the simplification of naturally occurring forms to their geometric essentials. **Paul** ________________

8. This French painter's ambition was to document the French countryside. To achieve it, he undertook a vast landscaping project including lily ponds. He painted water lilies for the next 20 years. **Oscar Claude** _____________

9. This French painter's works are noted for their vibrant light and often focus on people in intimate and candid compositions. **Pierre-Auguste** ______________

10. A French painter, sculptor, printmaker, ceramist and writer, his bold experimentation with colouring led to the Synthetist movement in which form and colour play an equal role. He is also known for Cloisonnism, the method of painting where the image is reduced to areas of pure colour separated by heavy black outlines. **Paul** __________________

11. A German-Swiss painter, he worked on, wrote and taught colour theory and form. His highly individualistic style reflects his musicality. **Paul** _______________

12. This Spanish painter was one of the most important painters of the Spanish Golden Age. He painted scenes of historical and cultural significance and portraits of the Spanish royal family, renowned European figures and commoners. **Diego** ________________

13. This Austrian painter was noted for his paintings, murals, sketches and other objets d'art. His primary subject was the female body and his works are erotic in nature. **Gustav** ________________

14. A Jewish Belarussian-French artist, he was a modernist. Distinguished by his use of colour in the works he created in almost every artistic medium, including paintings, book illustrations, stained glass, stage sets, ceramic, tapestries and fine-art prints. He also did large-scale paintings one of them being the ceiling of the Paris Opera. **Marc** _______________

15. A Catalan Spanish painter, sculptor and ceramicist, he was in favour of upsetting the visual elements of established painting. His work is considered a recreation of the childlike. **Joan** _____________

WHO WROTE IT?

Unscramble the author names and match these famous children's books to their authors.

Name of Book	Author	Unscrambled Name
1. Inkheart	a. NOIE FROLEC	____________
2. Sophie's World	b. MALES FALLGORE	____________
3. Comet in Moominland	c. ALICENOR KENUF	____________
4. Artemis Fowl	d. CORALS ZURI FANZO	____________
5. Babar the Elephant	e. ANJONAH RISPY	____________
6. The Wonderful Adventures of Nils	f. HIPPIL LAMPLUN	____________
7. Heidi	g. STONEJI DRAGARE	____________
8. His Dark Materials	h. OFAIB EGAD	____________
9. The Midnight Palace	i. VOTE SONJANS	____________
10. In the Sea There are Crocodiles	j. NAJE ED FROBHFUN	____________

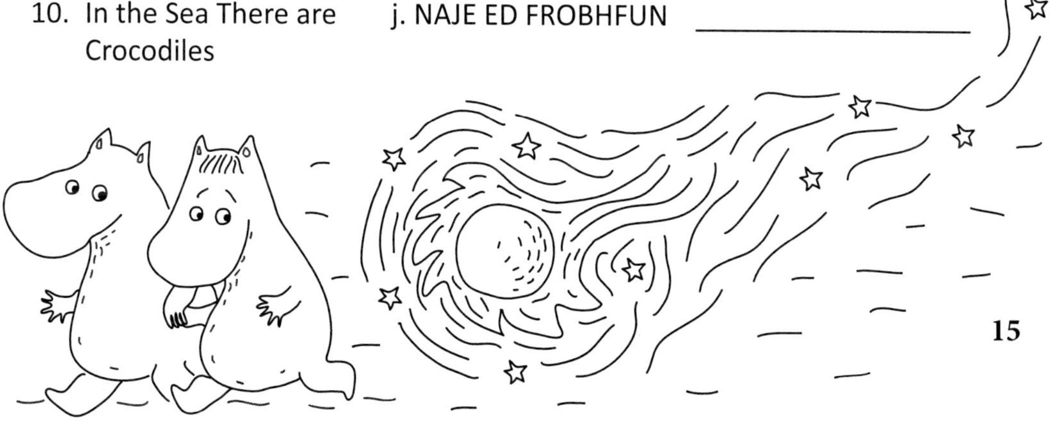

5

SAY CHEESE

Find the different kinds of cheese hidden in the following sentences:

1. This issue of the magazine Tricot talks about knits made of silk and wool-blended yarns.
2. The spinach should be blanched, darling.
3. The café tables are made of oak.
4. Maurice, Damascus is not the right holiday destination for us.
5. In the new system, men tally the liabilities while women tally the assets.
6. Margo, Udaipur is the perfect place for us to holiday.
7. I believe Calibri edges out every font.
8. Grandma's carp on English muffin is a special treat.
9. Seesaws tilt one way and then the other.
10. I request every Group Harmonica member to pay the annual subscription fees on time.

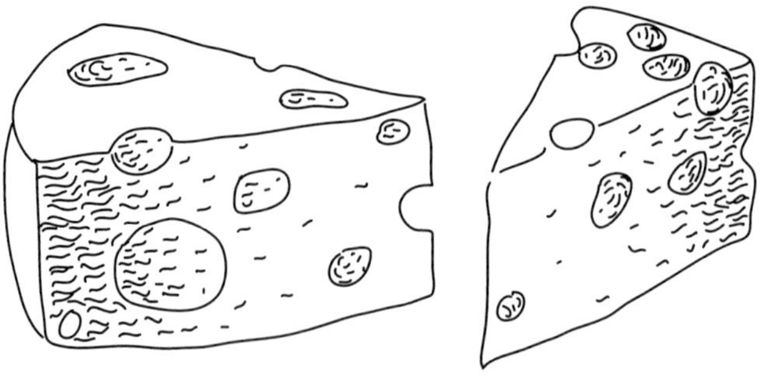

A RIVER RUNS THROUGH IT

Find the hidden European river running through each of the following sentences:

1. Can you spot five differences between these two pictures?
2. Steel beds are a design outrage.
3. If you hear "Code Red", you should drop what you're doing and head towards the fire escape.
4. Pierre, Gustav, Olga and Nadia have made it to the National Swimming Championships.
5. Isn't this hearth a mess?
6. There's the possibility of catarrh in every throat infection.
7. Hello, Irene. It's a pleasure to meet you.
8. You can tag us when you upload the picture to Facebook.
9. *Dear*, *honey* and *sweetheart* are common endearments.
10. Becoming a Sensei needs decades of training.

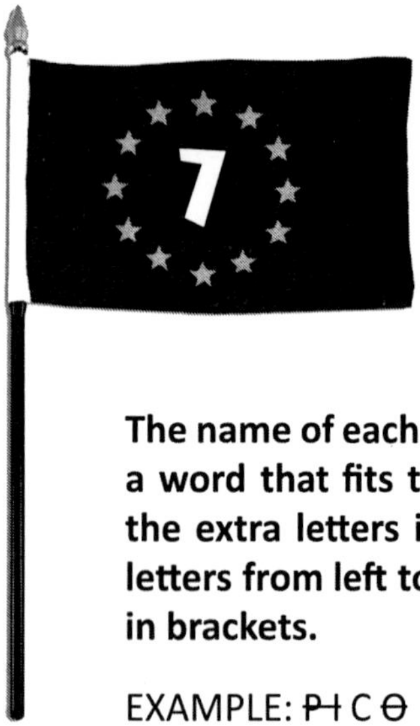

PEEK-A-PEAK

The name of each European peak in the left-hand column below contains a word that fits the clue given in that line. To find this word, cross off the extra letters in the mountain peak's name and read the remaining letters from left to right. The country to which this peak belongs is given in brackets.

EXAMPLE: ~~P I~~ C ~~O~~ A L M ~~A N Z O R~~ (Spain) Not stormy = CALM

Mountain Peak	**Clue**	**Answer**
Mount Bazarduzu (Russia)	Popular nickname for Shakespeare	________
Maja Jezerce (Albania)	Labyrinth	________
Mount Ossa (Greece)	Green growth in damp places	________
Corno Grande (Italy)	Thin rope	________
Puy de Sancy (France)	Senior official in a school, college or university	________
Torre de Cerredo (Spain)	What the judge says while banging his gavel	________
Snohetta (Norway)	What the nose excretes	________
Kebnekaise (Sweden)	A surface on which something rests	________
Gerlachovsky stit (Slovakia)	Two dozen	________
Hvannadalshnukur (Iceland)	A person who willfully destroys something	________

8

DIFFERENT BOOKS, COMMON THEME

Match the names of the novels in the first column with their authors in the second column. These novels have something in common. Do you know what it is?

Novel	**Author**
1. The Scarlet Pimpernel	a. Rafael Sabatini
2. A Tale of Two Cities	b. Daphne du Maurier
3. The Glass Blowers	c. Baroness Emma Orczy
4. The Duel	d. Anthony Burgess
5. Napoleon Symphony	c. Charles Dickens
6. Scaramouche	f. Joseph Conrad

VOWEL MUSIC

Add the missing vowels to identify the musical instruments that form a modern orchestra.

1. B _ S S _ _ N
2. T R _ M B _ N _
3. T R _ _ N G L _
4. _ B _ _
5. F L _ T _
6. V _ _ L _
7. C _ L _ S T _
8. G L _ C K _ N S P _ _ L
9. M _ R _ M B _
10. T _ B _

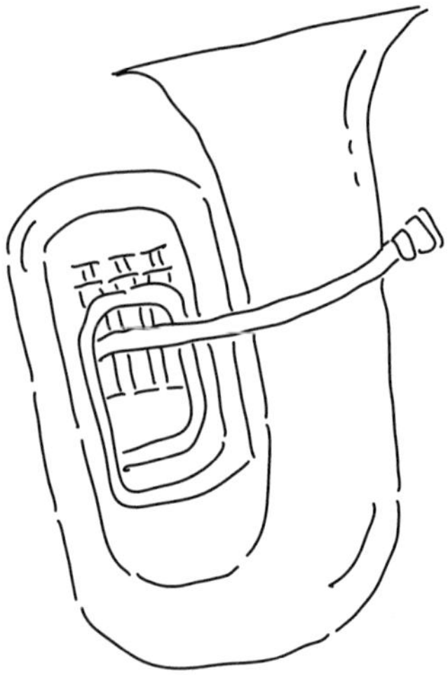

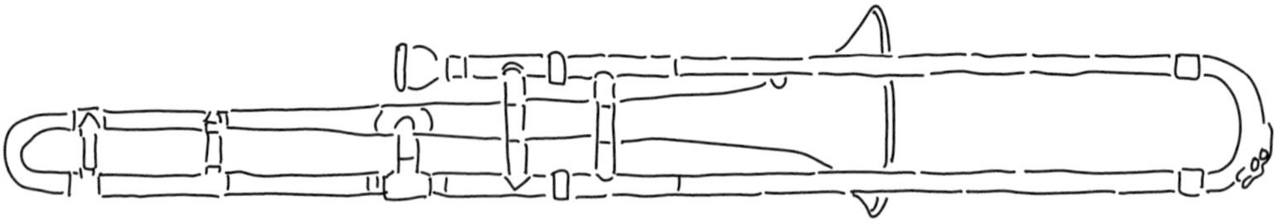

REVOLUTIONARY FACTS

Match the clues related to revolutions in Europe in the first column with their answers in the second column.

Clues	Answers
1. He was the ruler overthrown by the Russian Revolution	a. November 1917
2. An uprising across large parts of England in 1381	b. King William I
3. The Dutch War of Independence was fought against	c. Assault on the Bastille
4. The February Revolution of Russia took place in	d. Reign of Terror
5. The Greek Revolution (1821-32) was waged against	e. Peasants' Revolt
6. The Bolshevik Revolution took place in this month	f. 1641
7. A major event of the French Revolution	g. Nicholas II
8. The Irish Rebellion by Irish Catholics took place in	h. March 1917
9. The Belgian Revolution was an uprising against	i. Philip II of Spain
10. The period symbolised by the guillotine was called	j. The Ottoman Empire

MOVIE MAGIC

Match the names of the movies in the first column with their famous European directors in the second column.

Movie	**Director**
1. Three Colours Blue	a. Jean Renoir
2. Breathless	b. Dario Argento
3. Antichrist	c. Werner Herzog
4. The 400 Blows	d. Roman Polanski
5. Solaris	e. Krzysztof Kieślowski
6. The Rules of the Game	f. Ingmar Bergman
7. Rosemary's Baby	g. Andrei Tarkovsky
8. Signs of Life	h. François Truffaut
9. Suspiria	i. Jean-Luc Godard
10. The Seventh Seal	j. Lars Von Trier

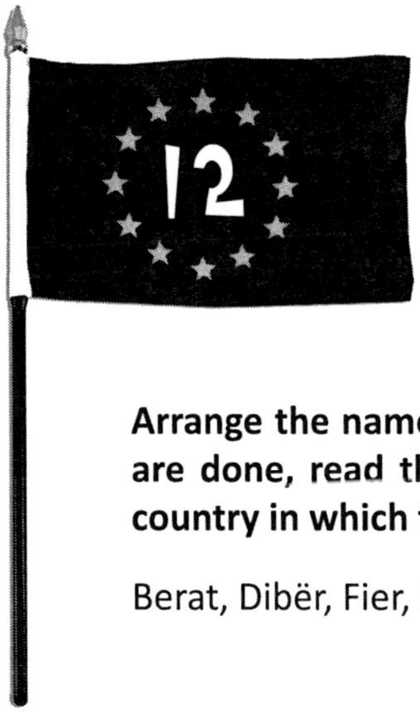

COUNTING COUNTIES

Arrange the names of the counties listed below into the grid. Once you are done, read the starred column top down to find the name of the country in which they are located.

Berat, Dibër, Fier, Elbasan, Gjirokastër, Tirana, Vlorë

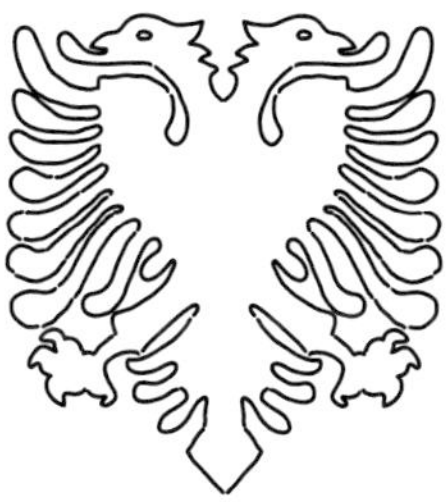

DICTATING TERMS

First, solve ALL the clues to identify the names of three famous European dictators. Then, insert the letters using the number code below each blank into the three sentences. Some of the blanks, which do not have number clues below them, are marked 'X'. See if you can fill in these blanks too to find a famous saying by each of the dictators.

1. His defeat in the Battle of Waterloo led to the phrase "he met his Waterloo", meaning "he lost", being included in the English language.

1 2 3 4 5 6 4 1   7 4 1 2 3 2 8 9 6

"13 14 3 4 16 16 13 7 5 6   13 16   2   X 4 8 10   11 4 15 1 10   4 1 5 X 13 1

9 12 6   10 13 X 9 13 4 1 2 8 X 4 11   11 4 4 5 16."

2. He is guilty of genocide on a mass scale.

2 10 4 5 11   12 13 9 5 6 8

“X 4 8 10 16   7 15 13 5 10   7 8 13 10 X 6 16   13 1 9 4

15 1 6 X 3 5 4   8 6 10   8 6 X 13 4 1 16.”

3. The Prime Minister of Italy who founded Fascism.

7 6 1 13 9 4   14 15 16 16 4 5 13 1 13

“7 6 9 9 6 8   9 4   5 13 X 6   2   10 2 X   2 16   2   5 13 4 1

9 12 2 1   2   12 15 1 10 8 6 10 X 6 2 8 16   2 16   2   16 12 6 6 3.”

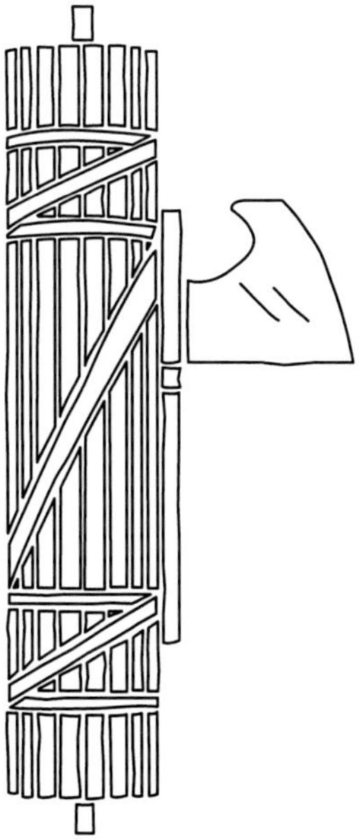

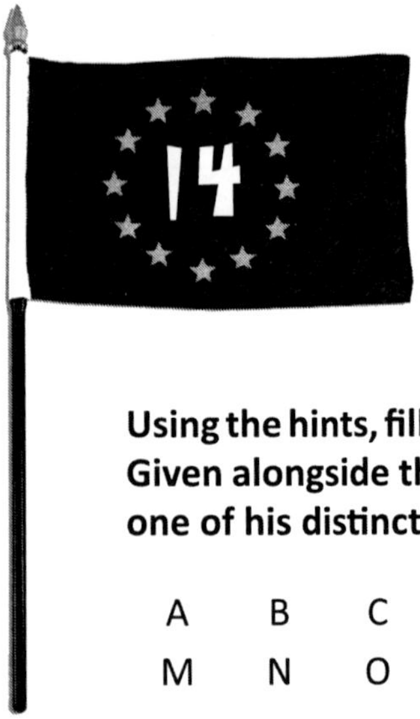

INTREPID EXPLORERS

Using the hints, fill in the blanks to guess the names of European explorers. Given alongside the explorer's name are the country he belonged to, and one of his distinctive achievements. Each letter is used only once.

A B C D E F G H I J K L

M N O P Q R S T U V Z

1. Rounded the southernmost tip of Africa and reached India in 1498. _ ASCO DA _A_A (Portugal)
2. He conquered the Incan empire for Spain and spread Spanish influence in South America. _RANC_SCO _I_ARRO (Spain)
3. He circumnavigated the globe between 1577-80, passing through the Strait of Magellan. SIR F_AN_IS DRA_E (England)
4. He led an expedition in 1534 up the St. Lawrence River as far inland as modern-day Montreal and established a presence for the French in modern-day Canada. _ AC_ _ ES CAR_I_R (France)
5. He was the first known European to cross the Mississippi River. _ERNAN_O DE _OTO (Spain)
6. He discovered the Pacific Ocean and the Isthmus of Panama in 1513. V_SC_ NU_EZ DE _A_BOA (Spain)

SIR WINSTON CHURCHILL SAID

Hidden in the grid below is a famous quote by Sir Winston Churchill, the Prime Minister of the United Kingdom from 1940-45 and 1951-55. Read across each row, from left to right, crossing out unnecessary letters to find it.

G	R	S	U	C	C	E	S	S	A	P	R	T	A	R
A	C	O	N	S	I	S	T	S	T	O	O	F	R	M
G	O	I	N	G	D	R	F	R	O	M	P	T	A	E
I	F	A	I	L	U	R	E	S	T	R	O	T	T	O
D	R	U	M	B	O	F	A	I	L	U	R	E	S	E
A	W	I	T	H	O	U	T	Y	L	O	S	S	O	F
T	O	U	L	S	E	N	T	H	U	S	I	A	S	M

16

THE INDUSTRIAL REVOLUTION

On the opposite page is a list of machines and manufacturing processes invented in Europe during the Industrial Revolution. Strike off the names on the list from the grid vertically (upward and downward), horizontally (forward and backward) and diagonally. Some letters may be crossed off more than once.

G	S	S	E	C	O	R	P	R	E	B	M	A	H	C	D	A	E	L	C
E	L	E	P	H	A	R	E	P	Q	R	S	T	A	M	M	A	T	R	O
R	T	H	R	E	S	H	I	N	G	M	A	C	H	I	N	E	B	L	T
M	I	L	E	E	N	I	H	C	A	M	G	N	I	L	L	I	M	C	T
S	E	E	D	D	R	I	L	L	D	L	B	A	E	V	L	T	Z	D	O
K	V	T	L	M	O	I	P	I	H	G	P	O	I	G	P	F	A	R	N
C	I	N	T	G	Y	E	N	M	R	L	B	L	E	A	C	H	I	N	G
Y	T	E	Y	A	G	N	L	S	A	O	P	S	A	T	O	L	U	S	I
P	O	M	R	S	S	O	N	T	F	A	N	R	T	T	T	G	M	T	N
H	M	E	I	L	E	R	H	E	T	A	R	P	E	N	E	O	S	E	E
I	O	C	G	I	G	E	N	A	J	U	S	O	L	F	A	M	N	A	M
Y	C	D	H	G	T	H	I	M	N	G	H	G	U	O	N	T	O	M	A
W	O	N	T	H	A	R	D	E	H	A	N	S	P	P	U	E	N	B	R
B	L	A	S	T	F	U	R	N	A	C	E	I	G	I	N	G	B	O	F
U	S	L	Q	I	T	W	E	G	C	A	N	N	N	N	O	T	H	A	R
G	L	T	U	N	U	A	R	I	A	N	T	E	E	N	I	B	L	T	E
W	O	R	I	G	H	A	T	N	W	I	L	L	H	A	I	Y	E	E	T
P	A	O	T	P	S	A	F	E	T	Y	L	A	M	P	S	P	L	D	A
E	N	P	C	Y	L	I	N	D	E	R	P	R	O	C	E	S	S	F	W
F	E	R	H	S	T	I	R	R	I	N	G	L	Y	P	O	E	T	I	C

1. Flying shuttle
2. Spinning jenny
3. Water frame
4. Cotton gin
5. Steam engine
6. Blast furnace
7. Lathe
8. Milling machine
9. Metal planer
10. Locomotive
11. Steam boat
12. Lead chamber process
13. Bleaching
14. Portland cement
15. Gas lighting
16. Cylinder process
17. Seed drill
18. Threshing machine
19. Iron plough
20. Safety lamp

FASHION A DESIGNER

Choose one letter from the letters given below and fill it into a blank such that the word forms the name of a fashion designer from a European country.

A	B	C	D	E	F	G	H	I	J	K	L	M
N	O	P	Q	R	S	T	U	V	W	X	Y	Z

1. TEU _ O LOMAN, Finland
2. HUSSEIN CHA _ AYAN, Cyprus
3. PACO RA _ ANNE, Spain
4. CATALIN BOTE _ ATU, Romania
5. BARBARA HULANIC _ I, Poland
6. _ INTS BUDE, Latvia
7. LUBICA KU _ EROVA, Slovakia
8. HEL _ UT LANG, Austria
9. _ ARYL KERRIGAN, Ireland
10. AGNETA ECK _ MYR, Sweden
11. GUNHILD N _ GAARD, Norway
12. ER _ E, Russia
13. CHRISTIAN LACROI _ , France
14. _ ILBERT DAS, Netherlands

15. HUGO B _ SS, Germany
16. JASPER CONR _ N, Britain
17. ELENA VOT _ I, Greece
18. _ ETER JENSEN, Denmark
19. ZIKA ASC _ ER, Czech Republic
20. _ ELIPE OLIVEIRA BAPTISTA, Portugal
21. FRANCO MOSCHI _ O, Italy
22. D _ IES VAN NOTEN, Belgium
23. KATERENA DEPAS _ UALE, Ukraine
24. ETIENNE A _ GNER, Hungary
25. JEAN-CHARLES DE CASTELBA _ AC, Morocco
26. ROBERT PIG _ ET, Switzerland

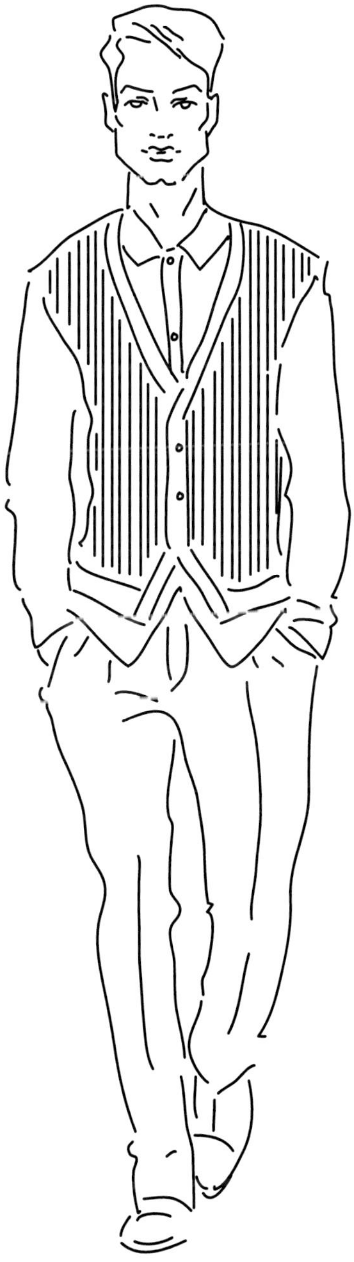

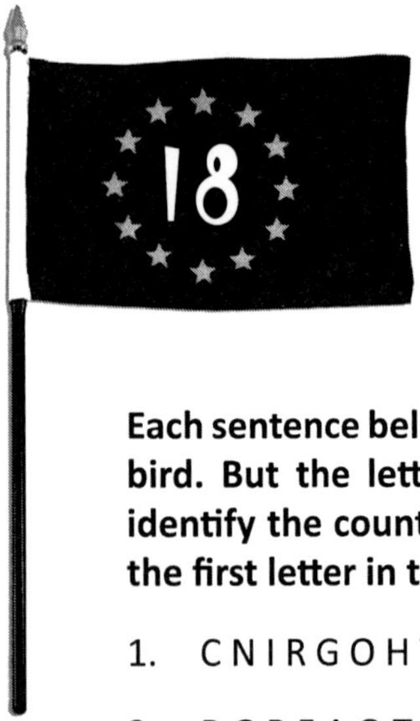

FEATHERED SYMBOLS

Each sentence below has the name of a European country and its national bird. But the letters have been mixed up. Can you separate them to identify the country and its national bird? The first letter in each clue is the first letter in the name of the country. Can you tell which is which?

1. C N I R G O H T I A N G A T L I E A
2. R G R E A O T W H I M T E P A E L I N C A N I A
3. L W I H I T E H S U T A O N R I K A
4. L G U O X L E D M C B R O E U S R T G
5. E B A R S N S W T A L O L N O I W A
6. I G O T L D E A N E A L G L Y E
7. G W H I E T E T R A I L E M D E A A G N L E Y
8. R T U U N D R S A S W S A I N A
9. U E N U I R T O E P E A D N K R O I B G R I N
10. G L I R T T L E E O E W C E L

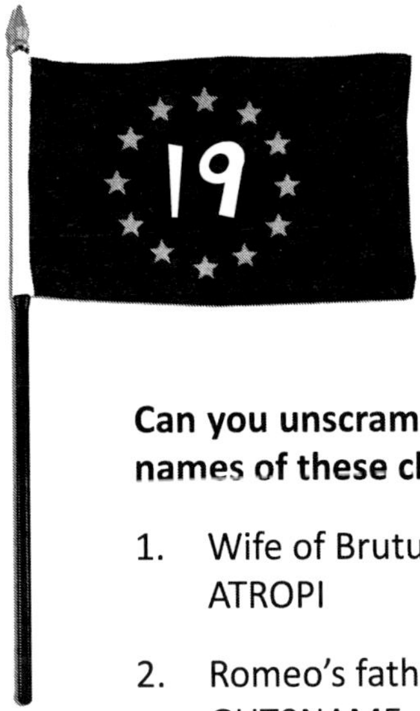

WHO ART THOU?

Can you unscramble the letters given alongside the clues to find out the names of these characters in Shakespeare's plays?

1. Wife of Brutus in *Julius Caesar* –
   ATROPI _ _ _ _ _ _

2. Romeo's father in *Romeo and Juliet* –
   GUTONAME _ _ _ _ _ _ _ _

3. Cymbeline's daughter in *Cymbeline* –
   GNOMEI _ _ _ _ _ _

4. Count of Rousillon in *All's Well That Ends Well* -
   ERRAMBT _ _ _ _ _ _ _

5. Son of the King of Scotland in *Macbeth* –
   COLLMAM _ _ _ _ _ _ _

6. Othello's wife in *Othello* –
   SEEDDAMNO _ _ _ _ _ _ _ _ _

7. Hamlet's mother in *Hamlet* –
   DRUGTREE _ _ _ _ _ _ _ _

8. A rich Jew moneylender in *The Merchant of Venice* –
   LOCHSKY _ _ _ _ _ _ _

9. Suitor of Katherina (Kate) in *The Taming of the Shrew* –
   UTRIPEOCH _ _ _ _ _ _ _ _ _

10. Daughter of Egeus in *A Midsummer Night's Dream* –
    RAMIEH _ _ _ _ _ _

20

HIDING FROM DANGER

Twenty endangered animals of Europe are hiding in this grid. Can you identify them? Look in all directions, backwards and forwards. Some letters are used more than once.

R	F	G	T	R	N	M	B	Q	T	P	E	L	M	A	N	I	S	M	A	B	E	C	L	P
N	O	R	T	H	A	T	L	A	N	T	I	C	R	I	G	H	T	W	H	A	L	E	R	S
V	B	A	N	L	Z	H	B	Q	F	P	A	D	M	N	F	T	Y	A	E	W	L	M	T	B
T	S	R	C	G	A	N	C	U	M	N	B	E	L	T	E	D	S	O	N	G	E	O	J	A
X	D	U	R	H	A	E	Z	N	A	V	E	R	B	O	T	E	B	B	E	S	R	N	K	V
N	D	D	E	E	S	C	R	R	I	E	C	E	R	T	I	B	N	H	E	S	T	T	W	A
Y	R	R	R	W	E	M	Y	Q	L	F	G	A	Y	B	Y	S	M	U	N	G	S	S	E	R
L	A	O	N	C	T	S	O	T	P	A	L	E	R	G	E	N	T	S	E	B	I	E	L	I
N	Z	S	U	A	H	A	J	U	R	O	O	L	A	L	A	M	B	O	U	R	P	N	R	A
A	I	U	R	R	A	I	U	E	S	M	M	G	U	N	S	T	A	M	E	N	I	Y	U	N
I	L	M	E	A	V	G	M	Q	S	E	S	N	R	B	M	F	L	I	X	E	P	B	C	P
R	K	W	I	B	B	A	B	M	T	T	T	D	E	R	S	I	F	T	Z	B	A	R	D	I
E	C	U	F	O	N	A	L	I	R	A	L	A	C	R	S	E	N	L	A	S	R	O	E	N
B	O	J	E	B	U	N	E	R	I	R	L	M	I	S	A	A	R	N	T	S	I	O	L	E
I	R	M	L	E	J	T	V	B	N	E	I	E	R	L	O	H	U	O	O	Q	E	K	L	V
M	N	U	T	E	K	E	E	S	G	L	B	L	U	W	E	Y	N	O	Z	W	D	N	I	O
A	A	Y	B	T	U	L	R	U	Y	O	C	L	M	Y	E	D	O	A	S	A	A	E	B	L
R	C	H	I	L	F	O	T	M	P	M	I	O	B	L	I	U	D	N	C	R	M	W	R	E
B	E	B	R	E	S	P	E	T	L	Y	T	W	I	E	R	C	H	O	I	I	E	T	E	I
L	U	O	C	A	S	E	X	I	O	D	N	D	Z	R	D	A	N	T	R	E	S	L	D	T
O	T	K	H	A	E	F	C	L	Y	N	A	Y	A	R	F	O	R	E	V	M	N	R	N	E
N	A	S	C	D	G	S	I	O	M	A	H	C	E	N	I	N	N	E	P	A	O	E	O	Y
T	B	F	I	G	U	N	E	T	F	S	R	S	L	O	P	M	Z	A	S	E	B	U	L	C
C	A	N	A	R	Y	L	O	N	G	E	A	R	E	D	B	A	T	C	R	A	F	T	S	Y
T	G	O	R	F	S	O	H	T	A	P	R	A	K	N	I	M	N	A	E	P	O	R	U	E

WHAT ARE YOU SAYING?

Match the names of these European languages with their dialects.

Language	**Dialect**
1. Lithuanian	a. Rauma
2. Portuguese	b. Chod
3. Spanish	c. Connacht
4. Russian	d. Bornholmian
5. Danish	e. Mirandese
6. Finnish	f. Epirote
7. Albanian	g. Samogitian
8. Greek	h. Masovian
9. Dutch	i. Leonese
10. Irish	j. Vologda
11. Hungarian	k. Friulian
12. German	l. Szekely
13. Italian	m. Gheg
14. Czech	n. Tweants
15. Polish	o. Ripuarian

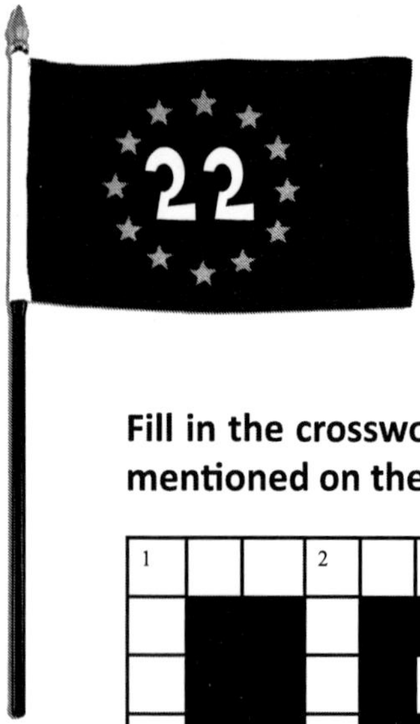

FAMOUS TITLES

Fill in the crossword with the titles of well-known books by the authors mentioned on the opposite page.

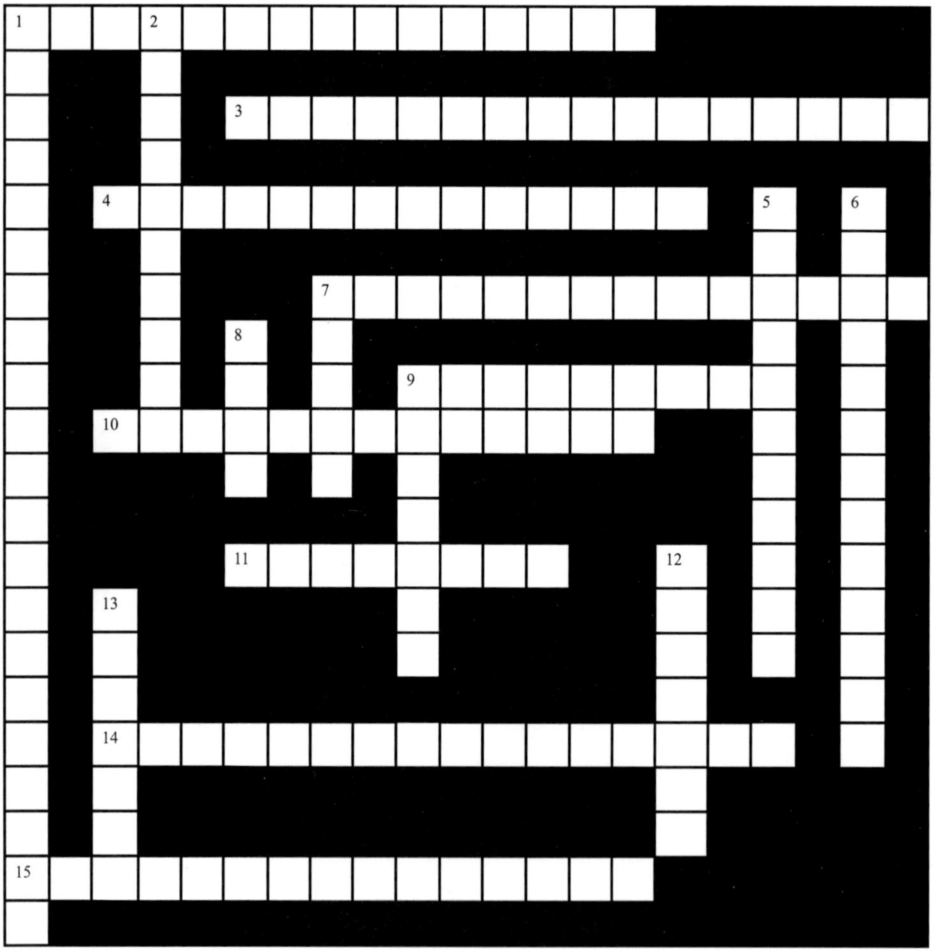

Across:

1. Dante Alighieri
3. Franz Kafka
4. Thomas Hardy
7. Ivan Turgenev
10. Victor Hugo
11. Molière
14. Charles Dickens
15. Frances Hodgson Burnett

Down:

1. Mikhail Bulgakov
2. Miguel de Cervantes
5. Virginia Woolf
6. A.A. Milne
7. Johann Wolfgang von Goethe
8. Jane Austen
9. Bram Stoker
12. William Shakespeare
13. Voltaire

23

FAIRYTALE CONFUSION

The fairytales of the Brothers Grimm and Hans Christian Andersen have travelled the world to become well-loved childhood stories. How well do you know these fairytales? Circle the correct answer from the options given.

1. Jack climbed the: oak tree, magic ladder, beanstalk, staircase
2. Hansel and Gretel left a trail of: breadcrumbs, confetti, glue, pebbles
3. The princess' body was so sensitive that she felt this thing that was kept under twenty mattresses: book, pea, stone, brick
4. Cinderella left this behind when she left the ball at midnight: glove, slipper, hairband, earring
5. Sleeping Beauty was awoken by: an injection, an electric current, a kiss, a magic incantation
6. Snow White's stepmother tried to kill her by giving her a poisoned: apple, orange, pear, cherry
7. Red Riding Hood noticed that the wolf had very large: whiskers, tail, eyes, feet
8. Rapunzel was known for her very long: eyelashes, fingernails, neck, hair
9. Goldilocks visited the bears' cottage and ate their: porridge, popcorn, pancakes, cornflakes
10. The Pied Piper of Hamelin rid the town of: ants, spiders, snails, rats
11. Pinocchio's nose grew longer every time he: cried, sighed, pried, lied
12. This animal threatened to huff and puff and blow the three little piggies' houses down: wolf, bear, elephant, lion

24

RHYME RIDDLES

Match the names of the nursery rhymes with their suspected historical origins.

Rhyme		**Historical Origin**	
1.	Ring a ring of roses	a.	In the 13th century, King Edward I imposed a tax on wool
2.	Here we go round the mulberry bush	b.	This cannon was used to gain control over the city of Colchester during the English Civil War
3.	Mary, Mary, quite contrary	c.	Protestant loyalists accused of plotting against Queen Mary I
4.	Baa, baa, black sheep	d.	Refers to the Great Plague of 1665
5.	Three blind mice	e.	This refers to how female prisoners exercised
6.	Humpty Dumpty sat on a wall	f.	The daughter of Henry VIII who gained a bad reputation for executing Protestant loyalists

ADDING UP SCIENCE

Join two letter groups from the box below to make the surnames (family names) of famous European scientists. You have two clues: the invention or discovery the scientist is famous for, and the country to which s/he belongs.

BEN	SCH	TOTLE	CUR	WRIGHT	LAVOI
NIE	MAR	USS	SSEN	CELLI	DAY
FLEM	RD	RONT	TZ	BAI	SIER
CONI	IE	JAN	EELE	MI	GEN
FARA	ARIS	CART	TORRI	ING	STRA

1. This German physicist discovered the X-ray.
2. This Italian physicist and mathematician invented the barometer.
3. This Greek philosopher and scientist performed a large-scale classification of plants and animals.
4. This German immigrant invented jeans.
5. This German businesswoman invented the coffee filter.
6. This Italian inventor is credited with the invention of radio.
7. This Polish chemist discovered radium.
8. This Scottish engineer invented the world's first fully electronic colour television tube.
9. This Scottish scientist invented penicillin.
10. This French scientist invented the bullet.

11. This Swedish scientist discovered chlorine.
12. This English inventor is credited with the power loom.
13. This French scientist discovered oxygen.
14. This Dutch scientist invented the compound microscope.
15. This British scientist discovered electromagnetic induction.

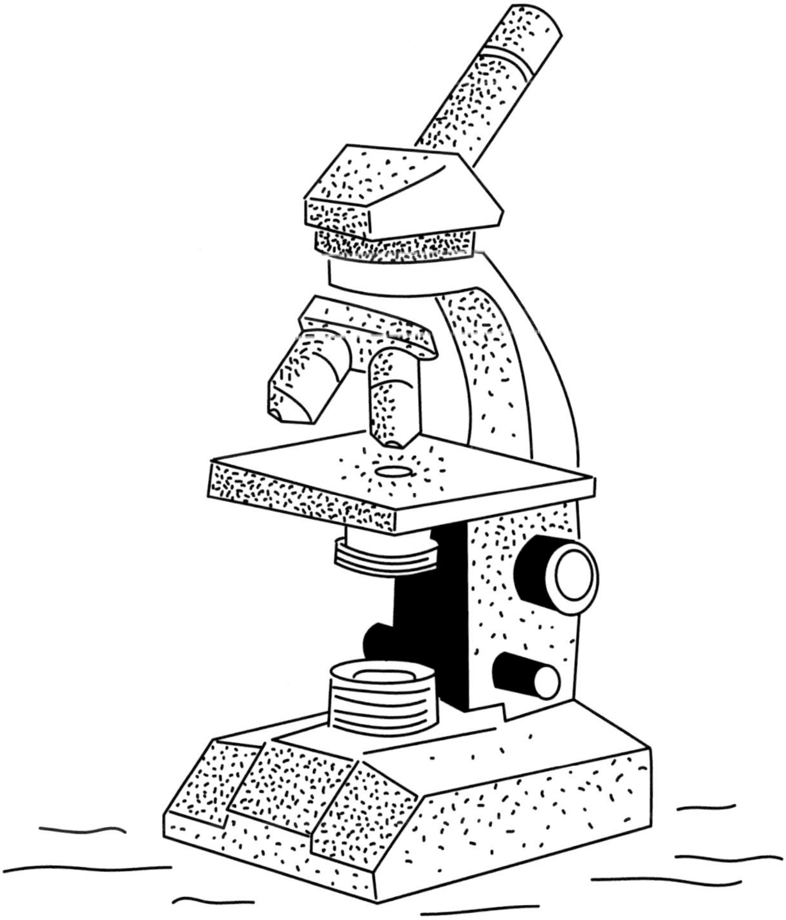

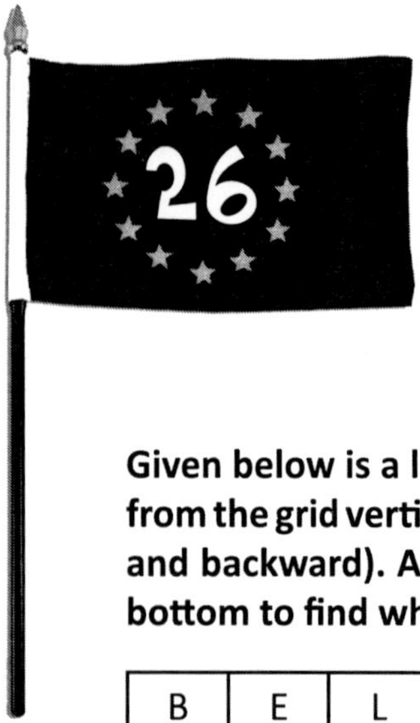

FIND THE COMMON THREAD

Given below is a list of towns and cities in Europe. Strike off their names from the grid vertically (upward and downward) and horizontally (forward and backward). Arrange the leftover letters from left to right and top to bottom to find what these places have in common.

B	E	L	U	S	H	Y	A	G	U	B	A
T	G	A	V	S	G	N	I	N	N	O	H
S	U	U	U	M	M	A	N	N	A	Q	T
E	P	H	T	M	A	E	Y	A	R	E	A
F	E	Q	U	U	G	N	O	S	K	I	D
R	R	A	I	R	N	O	R	I	L	S	K
E	N	A	M	M	A	T	R	O	M	S	O
M	A	N	I	A	T	B	O	V	E	T	H
M	V	A	S	N	A	E	A	R	C	T	I
A	I	A	I	S	H	C	T	I	K	S	I
H	K	Q	S	K	K	C	I	R	C	L	E
N	E	Y	B	R	A	E	Y	G	N	O	L

1. Longyearbyen (Norway)
2. Qaanaaq (Greenland)
3. Upernavik (Greenland)
4. Khatanga (Russia)
5. Murmansk (Russia)

6. Norilsk (Russia)
7. Tromso (Norway)
8. Sisimiut (Greenland)
9. Dikson (Russia)
10. Tiksi (Russia)
11. Belushya Guba (Russia)
12. Honningsvåg (Norway)
13. Uummannaq (Greenland)
14. Hammerfest (Norway)

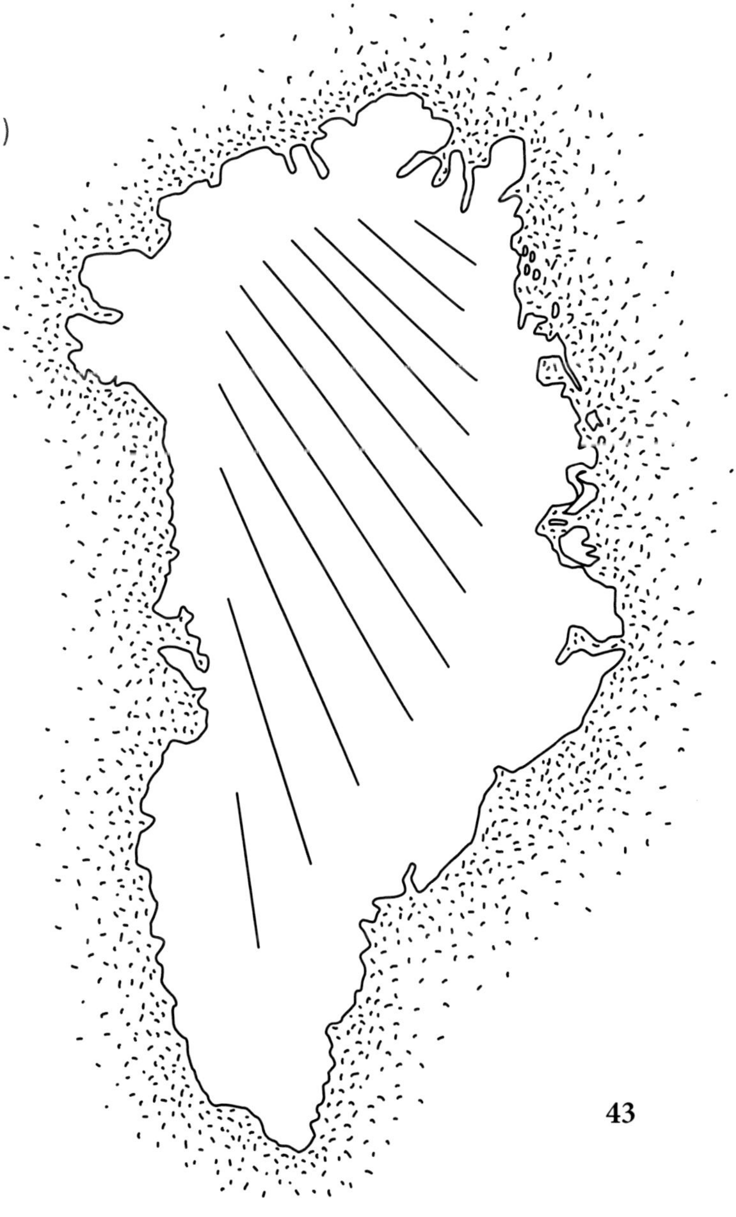

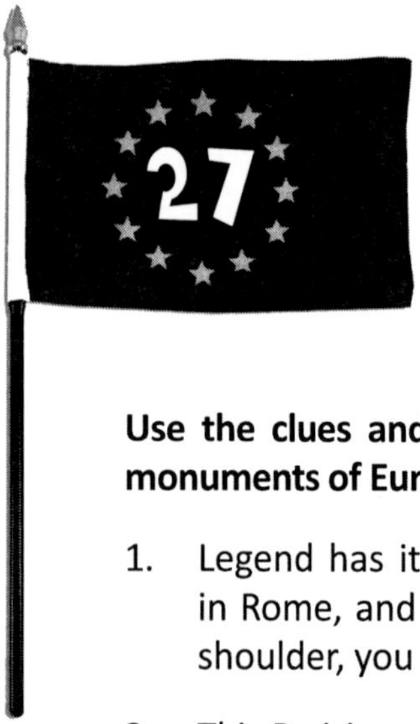

SIGHTSEEING

Use the clues and fill one letter in each blank to identify some famous monuments of Europe. Some vowels have been included to help you.

1. Legend has it that if you stand with your back to this place located in Rome, and throw a coin into it with your right hand over your left shoulder, you will one day return to Rome. _ _ _ _ I _ _ U _ _ A _ _
2. This Parisian monument commemorates those who died fighting in the French Revolution and the Napoleonic Wars. _ _ _ _ _ _ _ I _ _ _ _ E
3. A ring of massive stones constructed in England, this is Europe's oldest monument. _ _ O _ _ _ E _ _ _
4. This tall tower of iron in Paris is the most visited paid monument in the world. _ _ _ _ E _ _ O _ _ _
5. This building in Pisa, Italy is known for its ever-increasing tilt due to a poor foundation. _ _ A _ _ _ _ _ _ _ E _
6. The construction of this famous church in Barcelona began in 1882, but it is still incomplete today. _ _ _ A _ _ A _ _ _ _ _ I _ _ _
7. Located along the River Thames, this fortress has served as a royal residence, a prison and home to the Crown Jewels. _ _ _ _ _ O _ _ O _ _ _ _
8. This 2,500-year old temple located at the top of the Acropolis in Athens is still standing. _ A _ _ _ E _ _ _
9. A former city gate in Berlin, this is now a landmark of the reunification of Germany. _ _ A _ _ E _ _ _ _ _ _ A _ _
10. The world's largest amphitheatre in Rome was the arena for gladiators and public spectacles. _ _ _ O _ _ E _ _

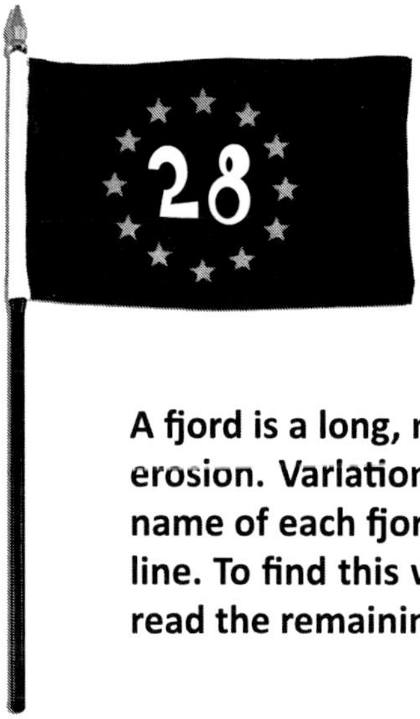

FORDING THE FJORDS

A fjord is a long, narrow inlet with steep sides or cliffs, created by glacial erosion. Variations in type and language create skerries and lochs. The name of each fjord below contains a word that fits the clue given in that line. To find this word, cross off the extra letters in the fjord's name and read the remaining letters from left to right.

EXAMPLE: L ~~Y~~ ~~S~~ E ~~F~~ ~~J~~ ~~O~~ ~~R~~ D, Norway   Past tense of the verb "lead" = LED

Fjord	Clue	Answer
1. Blindleia, Norway	The liver secretes this juice	________
2. Loch Etive, Scotland	An Asian species of onion	________
3. Scoresby Sund, Greenland	Spheres	________
4. Killary Harbour, Ireland	Hard work	________
5. Kola Bay, Russia	Place to conduct chemistry experiments	________
6. Eyjafjörður, Iceland	Double of the smallest even number	________
7. Schleswig-Holstein, Germany	This travels the fastest	________
8. Bohuslän, Sweden	Common public transport	________
9. Geirangerfjord, Norway	A warming spice	________
10. East Fjords, Iceland	You hear with them	________

WHO SOLVED IT?

Against each famous European crime novelist is a scrambled word. Unscramble each one to find the name of the detective s/he created.

1. Georges Simenon – SLEJU GREATIM _ _ _ _ _ _ _ _ _ _ _ _
2. Henning Mankell – URTK LAWDARLNE _ _ _ _ _ _ _ _ _ _ _ _ _
3. Steig Larsson – KALEMI SKOLIVTMB _ _ _ _ _ _ _ _ _ _ _ _ _ _ _
4. Dorothy L. Sayers – TREEP MEWSYI _ _ _ _ _ _ _ _ _ _ _
5. Edmund Crispin – SAVERGE ENF _ _ _ _ _ _ _ _ _ _
6. G.K. Chesterton – THRAFE WRONB _ _ _ _ _ _ _ _ _ _ _
7. Ian Rankin – HJNO BRUSE _ _ _ _ _ _ _ _ _
8. Manuel Vázquez Montalbán – EPPE HARLOCAV _ _ _ _ _ _ _ _ _ _ _ _
9. P D James – MAAD SLADEILGH _ _ _ _ _ _ _ _ _ _ _ _ _
10. Andrea Camilleri – LOVAS LABTONANOM _ _ _ _ _ _ _ _ _ _ _ _ _ _ _

DID YOU KNOW?

Here are some interesting facts about some European countries. Can you identify the country by the clues?

1. No location in this country is farther than 52 km from the coast.
2. This country has the northernmost capital in the world.
3. This is the smallest internationally recognised independent state in the world, in both area and population.
4. The national language of this country is the only Semitic language to be officially recognised by the European Union.
5. This country has the oldest national flag in Europe.
6. This tiny country in Europe claims to be the oldest state in Europe, having been founded in the 4th century.
7. This independent principality in the Pyrenees is co-governed by the President of France and Spain's Bishop of Urgel.
8. This sovereign city-state has the highest population density in Europe and the world's lowest unemployment rate.
9. This tiny republic comprises islands, of which only three are inhabited.
10. This is the only country in the world to lie entirely in the Alps.

GODS WITH JOBS

The names of 15 Greek and Roman gods and goddesses have been broken up in three letter-groups. Match a letter group in Column A with letters in Columns B and C to complete the name of a mythological figure. Then, match the names with what the gods and goddesses are known for. Can you tell which ones are Greek and which are Roman?

	A	B	C	Name		God (dess) of
1.	MI	CH	LO		a.	Time
2.	AP	TU	IS		b.	Love
3.	APH	TEM	NE		c.	Hunt
4.	BAC	OL	RN		d.	Wisdom
5.	HEPH	TU	ITE		e.	Sun
6.	SA	RM	US		f.	Fire
7.	DE	AES	ER		g.	Wine
8.	HE	NER	TUS		h.	Travel
9.	NEP	ROD	VA		i.	Sea
10.	AR	MET	ES		j.	Grain

NORSE MYTHOLOGY

Norse Mythology divides the earth into three worlds. Fill in the blanks to make fruits and vegetables. Then, read down the blanks to find the names of the three Norse worlds.

_ PPLE	_ ANGO	_ ECTARINE
_ TARFRUIT	_ VY GOURD	_ CEBERG LETTUCE
_ UAVA	_ URIAN	_ IG
_ PRICOT	_ RAPES	_ YCHEE
_ AISINS	_ VOCADO	_ ORSERADISH
_ ATES	_ ASPBERRY	_ GGPLANT
	_ RUMSTICK	_ NDIAN PEA
		_ USK MELON
________________	________________	________________
(where the gods lived)	(the world of men)	(the world of the dead)

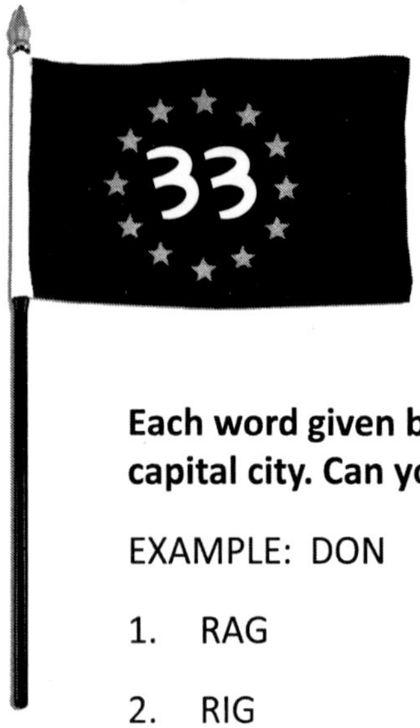

MAIN BITS

Each word given below is contained in the name of a European country's capital city. Can you identify these capitals?

EXAMPLE: DON LONDON

1. RAG
2. RIG
3. LET
4. HIS
5. CHAR
6. RAT
7. THE
8. PEN
9. COW
10. POD
11. RAN
12. RID
13. ALL
14. PAR
15. APE

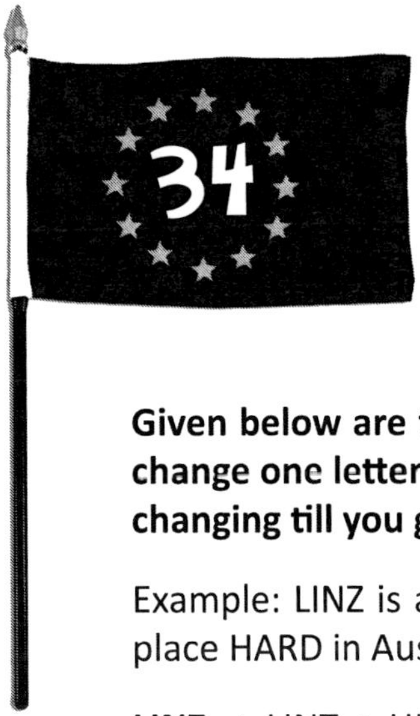

FROM HERE TO THERE

Given below are the names of some European towns. With each name, change one letter at a time to form a word in the English language. Keep changing till you get to the town at the end.

Example: LINZ is a place in Austria, and you need to change it to get the place HARD in Austria.

LINZ -> LINT -> HINT -> HIND -> HAND -> **HARD** (Austria)

C O R K (Ireland)	P O R I (Finland)	S A L O (Finland)
_ _ _ _	_ _ _ _	_ _ _ _
_ _ _ _	_ _ _ _	_ _ _ _
_ _ _ _	_ _ _ _	_ _ _ _
S I O N (Switzerland)		M O S T (Czech Republic)
	_ _ _ _	
	H V A R (Croatia)	

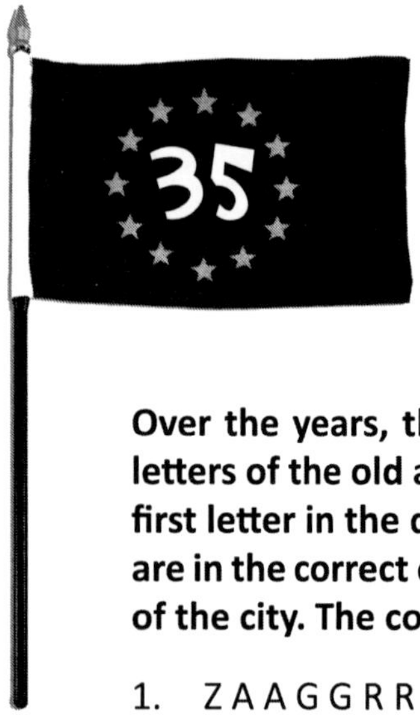

CHANGING CITY NAMES

Over the years, the names of some European cities have changed. The letters of the old and new names of cities have been mixed together. The first letter in the question is the present name of the city, and the letters are in the correct order. Separate the letters to find the old and new name of the city. The country in which the city is located is given in brackets.

1. Z A A G G R R A E B M (Croatia)

   New name: ____________________ Old Name: ____________________

2. N G O U D T U H A A K B (Greenland)

   New name: ____________________ Old Name: ____________________

3. T R A E V L E L I L N N (Estonia)

   New name: ____________________ Old Name: ____________________

4. S A R T G E N R T O A R S B A O T U R U M G (France)

   New name: ____________________ Old Name: ____________________

5. P L U A T E R T I I S A (France)

   New name: ____________________ Old Name: ____________________

6. B F E O L L S O G I N A N A (Italy)

   New name: ____________________ Old Name: ____________________

7. P T I T O O D G G O R I R A C D A (Montenegro)

   New name: ____________________ Old Name: ____________________

8. M T R A A I A S E T C R T I U C H M T (Netherlands)

New name: ____________________ OldName:__________________

9. G D A N D A N Z S I G K (Poland)

New name: ____________________ OldName:__________________

10. S P A I N E T P T E R T E O R S G B U R R A D G (Russia)

New name: ____________________ OldName:__________________

11. U O S P T R A P A S R A O L S A (Sweden)

New name: ____________________ OldName:__________________

12. O H A D C E S I B S E Y A (Ukraine)

New name: ____________________ OldName:__________________

13. Y S V E K E A R T E D L R I O N B V U S R K G (Russia)

New name: ____________________ OldName:__________________

14. B K R O R N S A T A S D O T V (Romania)

New name: ____________________ OldName:__________________

15. L O L I I S S B I O P O N (Portugal)

New name: ____________________ OldName:__________________

GYPSY RHYTHMS

The names of some European gypsy tribes have been listed below. Place each name in the middle of a 'word box' so that you have three-letter words when you read the letters top down. You can only use four of the tribe names.

Sinti	Manush	Erlides	Romungro
Bosha	Boyash	Churari	Machvaya

A P A A H
_ _ _ _ _
H N D E D

A F B R A S
_ _ _ _ _ _
S R E G K E

M I A R A R U
_ _ _ _ _ _ _
T E L M O D E

C R I R E E A T
_ _ _ _ _ _ _ _
Y D P E D O T E

37 A-MAZE-ING SCRIPTS

Hidden in the grid below are the names of 24 European scripts. Can you find them? Read horizontally, vertically and diagonally, to find them. A letter may be used more than once.

F	L	E	M	I	S	H	U	N	G	A	R	I	A	N
I	I	B	A	T	D	S	P	R	F	R	V	A	O	A
N	T	G	C	H	S	I	L	O	P	G	E	R	F	M
N	H	C	E	Z	C	D	E	M	K	O	W	E	H	R
I	U	D	D	I	M	E	S	A	P	E	L	C	K	E
S	A	Y	O	T	X	W	C	N	G	I	T	I	L	G
H	N	N	N	A	N	S	Z	I	D	U	B	D	S	O
S	I	A	I	L	C	R	A	A	D	T	J	N	E	H
I	A	I	A	I	W	N	P	N	A	Q	U	A	R	S
N	N	V	N	A	I	T	A	O	R	C	T	L	B	I
A	H	O	R	N	A	I	S	S	U	R	I	E	I	L
P	C	D	E	F	L	O	I	P	B	T	H	C	A	G
S	T	L	S	L	O	V	E	N	I	A	N	I	N	N
P	U	O	S	T	I	N	N	A	I	N	O	T	S	E
I	D	M	A	M	B	E	N	A	I	N	A	R	K	U

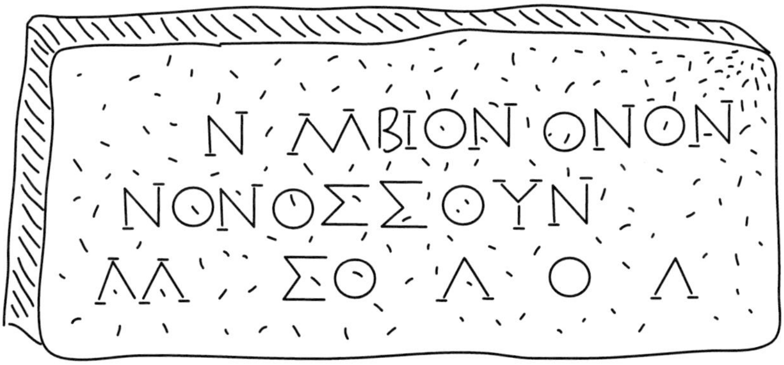

STARRY FAME

Can you unscramble the letters below to identify these prominent European actresses? Your clues are the movies for which they are famous (in italics), and the country in which they were born.

1. *Casablanca*, Sweden – GRINDI MANGERB _ _ _ _ _ _ _ _ _ _ _ _ _
2. *El Cid*, Italy – PAISHO ELNOR _ _ _ _ _ _ _ _ _ _ _
3. *Gone With the Wind*, India – IVINEV HIGEL _ _ _ _ _ _ _ _ _ _ _
4. *Contempt*, France – BITTERIG TODRAB _ _ _ _ _ _ _ _ _ _ _ _ _ _
5. *Skyfall*, United Kingdom – UIJD CEHND _ _ _ _ _ _ _ _ _
6. *Doctor Zhivago*, India – ULEJI CHESTIRI _ _ _ _ _ _ _ _ _ _ _ _ _
7. *Miracle on 34th Street*, Ireland – NAMERUE AROHA _ _ _ _ _ _ _ _'_ _ _ _
8. *Breakfast at Tiffany's*, Belgium – UREADY PUNHERB _ _ _ _ _ _ _ _ _ _ _ _ _
9. *Sissi*, Austria – OYRM HINDSCERE _ _ _ _ _ _ _ _ _ _ _ _ _
10. *Europa*, Germany – ARABBAR WUSAKO _ _ _ _ _ _ _ _ _ _ _ _ _

DOUBLE DATE TROUBLE

Given below are events that occurred in Europe, with two years given against each. Tick the correct year, when the event actually occurred.

1. Rome (called Roma then) was founded by Romulus. 753 BC / 776 BC
2. Christopher Columbus discovered America. 1526 / 1492
3. France was proclaimed a republic. 1792 / 1794
4. The USSR was created. 1925 / 1922
5. The Channel Tunnel, a railway line under the English Channel linking the United Kingdom with France, opened. 1988 / 1994
6. The Portuguese explorer Vasco da Gama reached India. 1498 / 1499
7. Czechoslovakia separated into two countries: the Czech Republic and Slovakia. 1989 / 1993
8. Nicolae Ceausescu, the Romanian dictator, was executed. 1989 / 1991
9. A nuclear accident occurred at the Chernobyl Nuclear Power Plant in Ukraine. 1989 / 1986
10. The Euro came into existence as currency in this year. 1999 / 1995

RED, WHITE AND BLUE

The flags below are of European countries, both present and past. Can you identify the countries to which these flags belong? Fill one letter in each blank.

1. 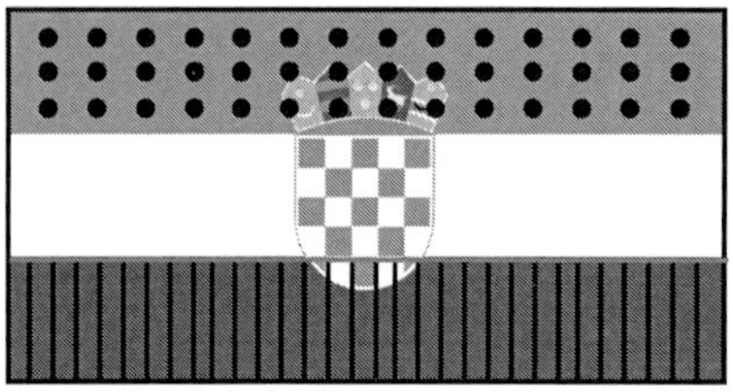

_ _ _ _ _ _ _

2. 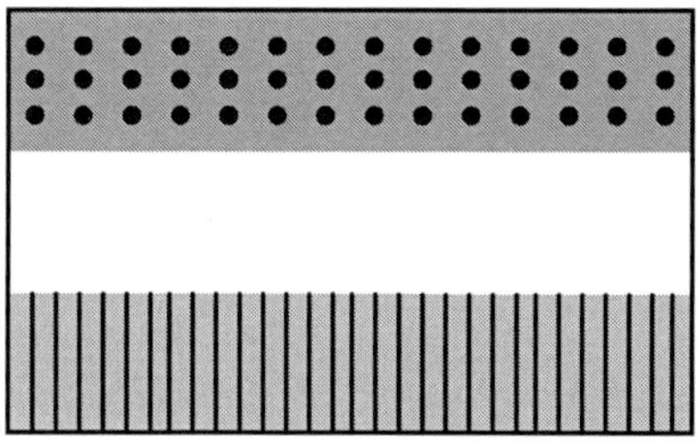

_ _ _ _ _ _ _ _ _ _

3. 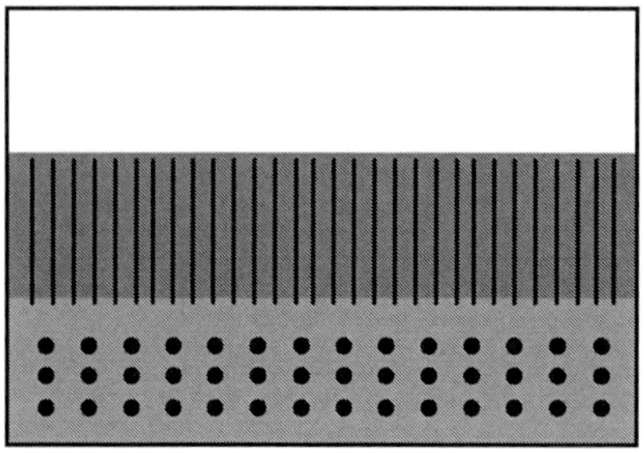

_ _ _ _ _ _

4. 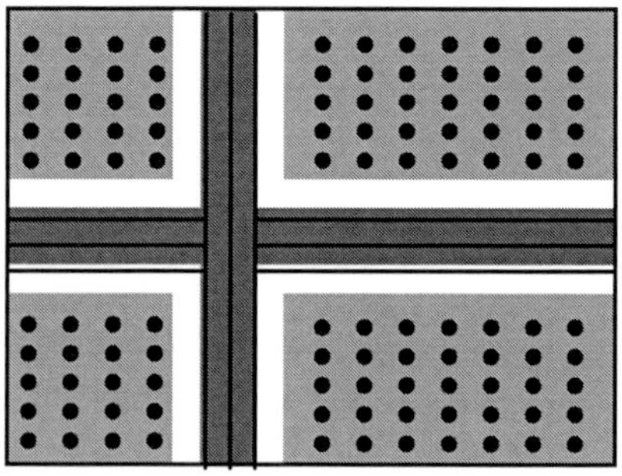

_ _ _ _ _ _

KEY

All stripes denote the colour blue.

All dots denote the colour red.

All blank spaces denote the colour white.

5. 

6. 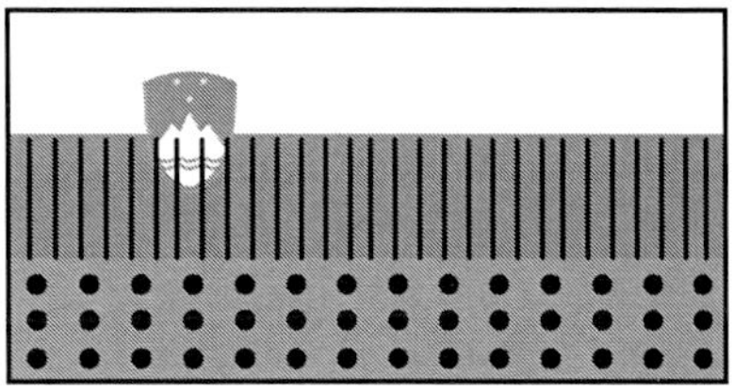

_ _ _ _ _ _ _ _   _ _ _ _ _ _ _ _ _ _

_ _ _ _ _ _ _ _ _ _ _

7. 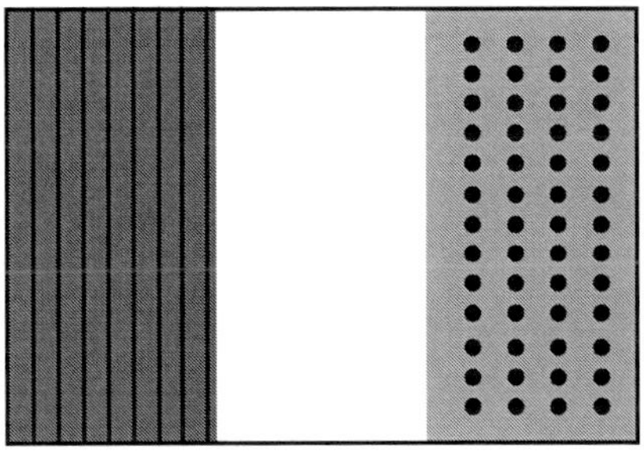

8. 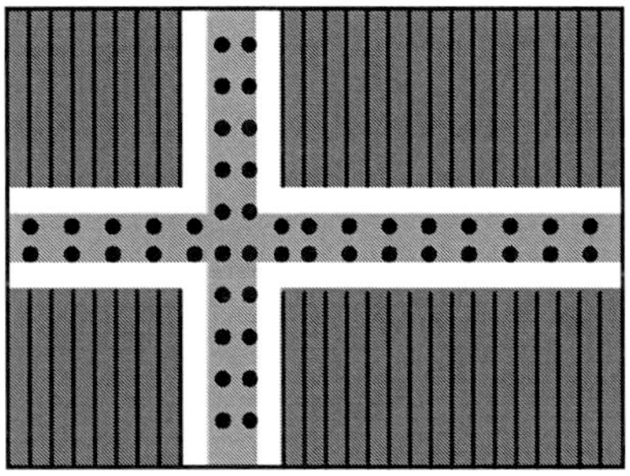

_ _ _ _ _ _ _ _

_ _ _ _ _ _ _ _ _ _

9. 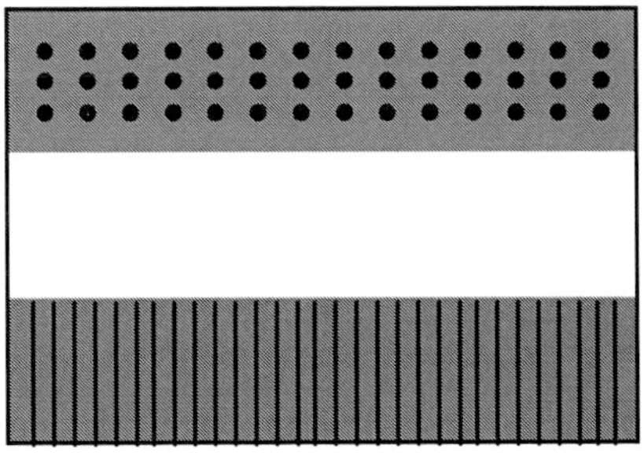

10. 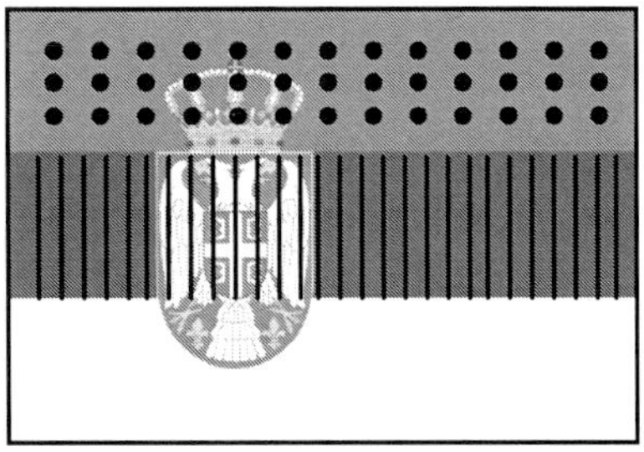

_ _ _ _ _ _ _ _ _ _ _ _ _ _ _

_ _ _ _ _ _ _ _

NOW YOU SEE IT, NOW YOU DON'T!

Find the European city hidden in the following sentences:

1. Alice rubbed her eyes as she saw the vermin skate past her.
2. Vladimir Ilyich is in Austria? No!
3. Avanti ran away before the bear could attack her.
4. Mr Micawber lingered over the dessert; it was delicious.
5. 'Give nice Mrs Green a kiss, Peter,' said Mrs Darling.
6. Did you know that gene variations can result in entirely different species of beings?
7. Emilio and Marco log nearly three hours in the gym every day.
8. Go slowly on the slopes because you're not really ready yet.
9. Sometimes, evil leaves us all feeling diminished.
10. The wombat has a short, stubby tail.
11. The ailing hen thrashed around.
12. Some people acknowledge Noah's contribution to the perpetuation of various species.
13. Little Nimmo scowled when her father refused to give her any more candy.
14. This carousel is bonded to the central pole with industrial-strength glue.
15. Ahmad, rid this city of these pestilential mice, and I will pay you handsomely.

THE EUROPEAN UNION

Strike off the names of 15 countries that are members of the European Union (EU) from the grid—vertically (upward and downward) and horizontally (forward and backward). A letter may be used more than once. Arrange the leftover letters from left to right, from the top row to the bottom row, to find the names of four European countries that are <u>not</u> members of the EU.

A	I	N	A	M	O	R	D	A	I	V	T	A	L
L	C	Z	E	C	H	R	E	P	U	B	L	I	C
G	E	R	M	A	N	Y	N	E	C	E	E	R	G
E	I	N	C	H	T	E	M	S	W	E	D	E	N
N	A	I	R	T	S	U	A	T	S	T	E	I	N
D	N	A	L	N	I	F	R	O	M	A	L	T	A
R	U	P	S	S	I	A	K	N	Y	L	A	T	I
N	O	S	L	O	V	E	N	I	A	R	W	A	Y
S	E	P	O	R	T	U	G	A	L	R	B	I	A

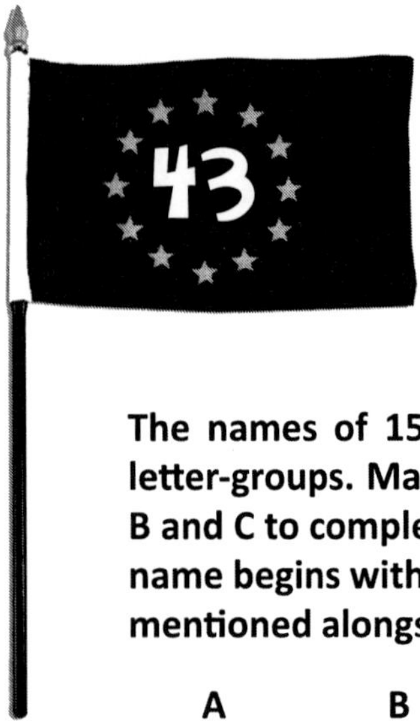

PORTER

The names of 15 European port cities have been broken up in three letter-groups. Match a letter group in Column A with letters in Columns B and C to complete the name of the port city. Your clue is that the city's name begins with the letters in column A, and it is located in the country mentioned alongside.

	A	B	C	Capital		Country
1.	LEH	TWE	IN	___________	a.	France
2.	PI	ERHA	DAM	___________	b.	Greece
3.	DU	TER	OKK	___________	c.	Ireland
4.	ROT	PEZ	RE	___________	d.	Netherlands
5.	AN	ECI	OWE	___________	e.	Belgium
6.	ALG	IXST	RP	___________	f.	Spain
7.	BREM	AV	US	___________	g.	Germany
8.	LAS	BL	RAS	___________	h.	Italy
9.	FEL	AXL	IA	___________	i.	United Kingdom
10.	MARS	RAE	VEN	___________	j.	Malta

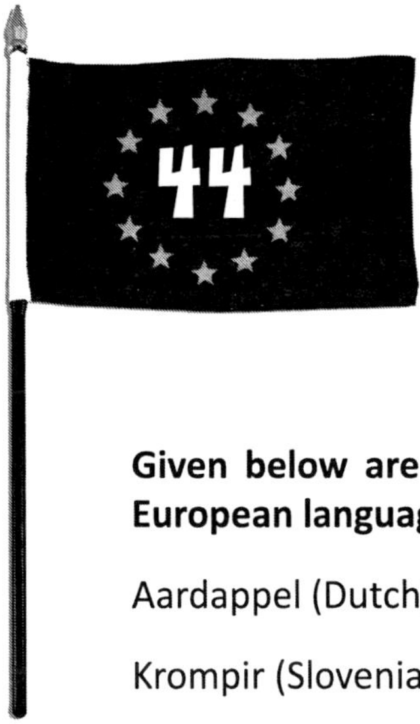

A VEGETABLE BY ANOTHER NAME

Given below are the names of vegetables as they are called in some European languages. Can you guess which vegetable it is?

Aardappel (Dutch)

Krompir (Slovenian)

Brambor (Czech)

Ziemniak (Polish)

Kartoffel (Danish)

Burgonya (Hungarian)

Kartoflu (Icelandic)

Bulves (Lithuanian)

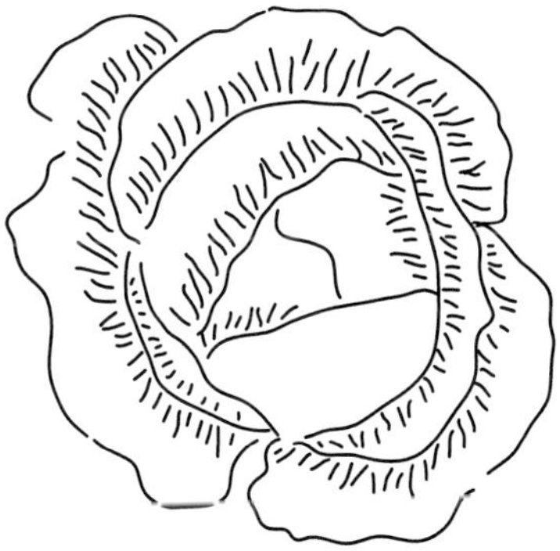

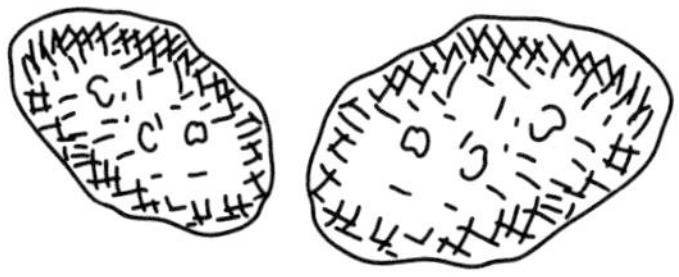

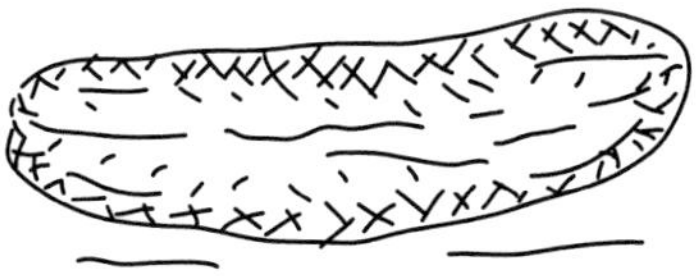

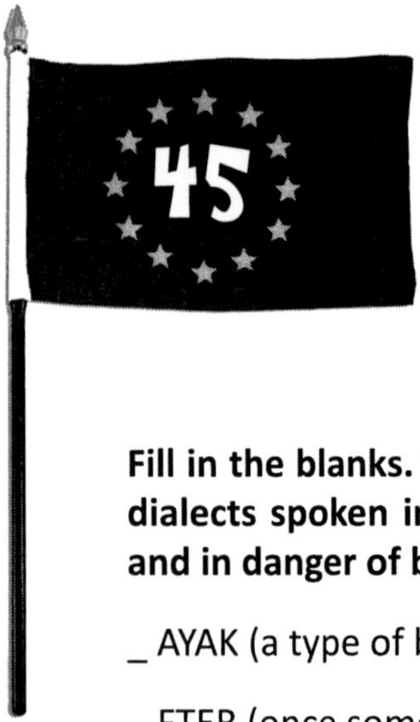

HOW GREEN IS MY LAND!

Fill in the blanks. Then, read down the blanks to get the names of three dialects spoken in Greenland. They are very different from each other, and in danger of becoming extinct.

_ AYAK (a type of boat)
_ FTER (once something is over)
_ IFT (to pick up)
_ LTER (to change)
_ NGER (strong annoyance)
_ IMB (arm or leg)
_ IGHT (you need it to read by)
_ NK (blue liquid you write with)
_ TAIN (mark left by something)
_ NDER (opposite of 'over')
_ RAIN (it has an engine and a whistle)

_ RUNK (chest made of metal)
_ RBAN (opposite of 'rural')
_ EVER (no, not again!)
_ LSTER (a type of overcoat)
_ ISER (stingy with money)
_ NNER (not outer)
_ RATE (very angry)
_ TUN (shock into immobility)
_ KELELE (stringed musical instrument)
_ RASH (rubbish)

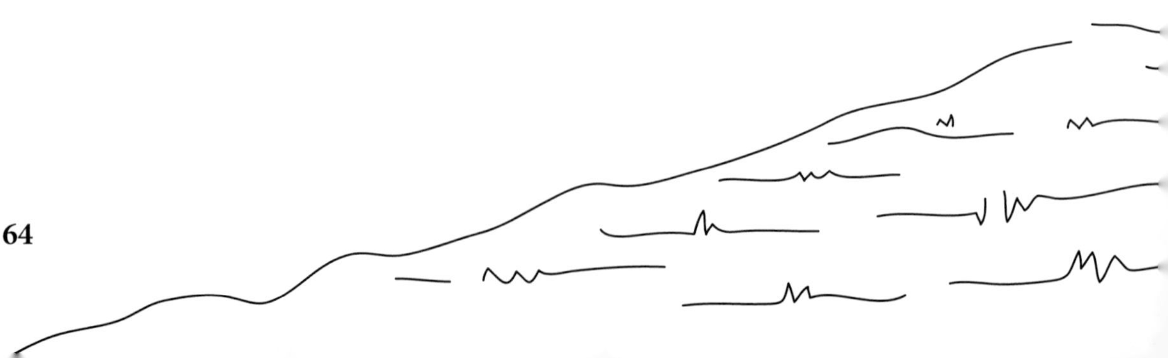

_ MAGE (picture)

_ OBLE (a gas, or a member of the upper class)

_ NIFORM (police officers and guards wear them)

_ NIT (how to make a sweater)

_ EMPO (speed at which music is played)

_ NITY (being together)

_ ARROW (of small width)

____

IT'S COMPLICATED

Put the names of the municipalities listed below into the grid using the number of letters as a clue. Once you are done, read down the starred column to find the name of the country in which they are located. Hint: It is a self-governing country within the Danish Realm.

Eioi (4) Hov (3) Hvalba (6) Nes (3) Sandur (6) Sumba (5)

Famjin (6) Husar (5) Kunoy (5) Runavik (7) Tórshavn (8) Vestmanna (9)

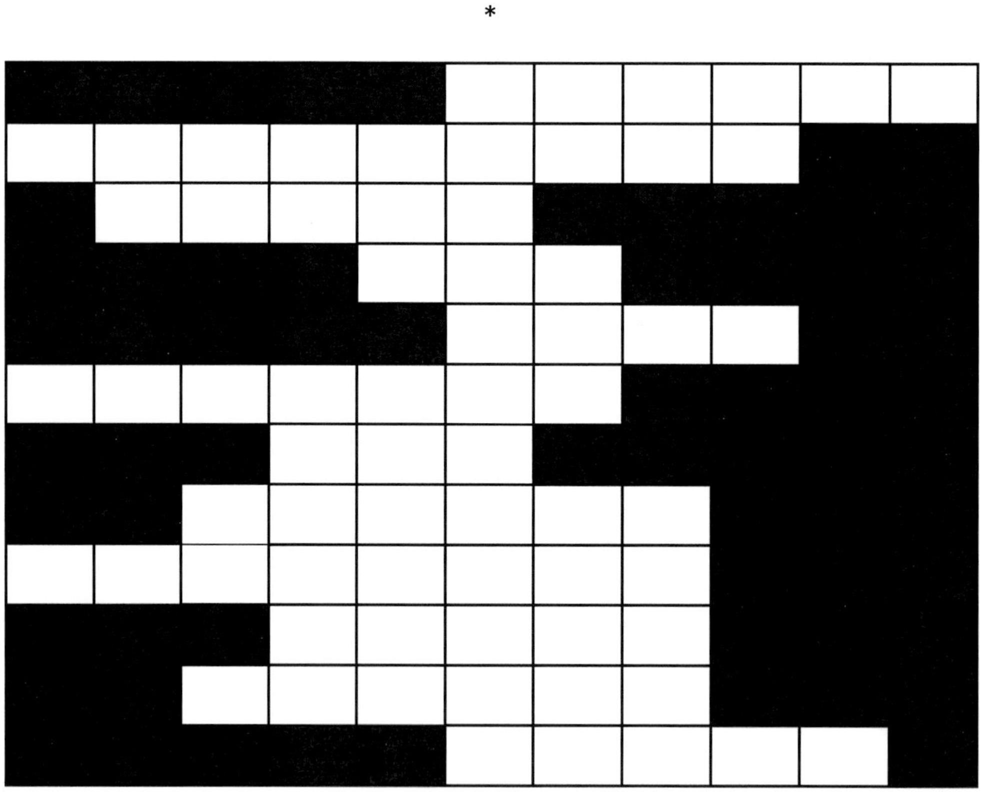

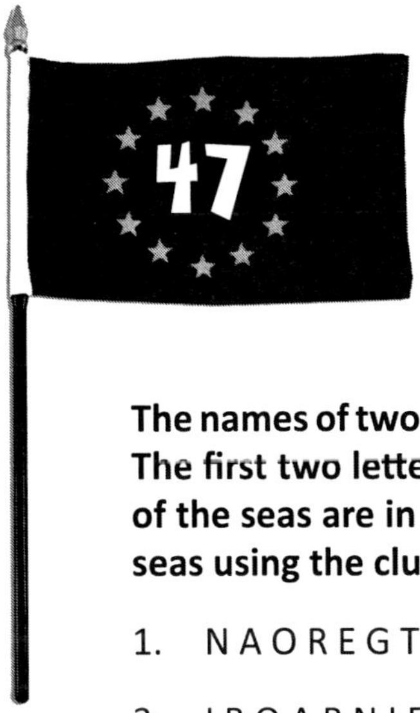

MIXED-UP WATERS

The names of two European seas are mixed up in each sequence of letters. The first two letters are the first letters of each of these seas. The letters of the seas are in the correct order. Can you separate them? Identify the seas using the clues given.

1. N A O R E G T E A H N _______________ and _______________
2. I B O A R N I E N A T N S _______________ and _______________
3. L B I A G L U T R I I A C N _______________ and _______________
4. I A R D R I I S A T I H C _______________ and _______________
5. W N H O R I W E T G I A E N _______________ and _______________

48 NATIONAL TIDBITS

Here are some interesting facts about some European countries. Can you identify the countries by the clues?

1. This country's national colour is not on its national flag.

   ____

2. Two European countries share the apple as their national fruit. Name them. ________ and ________

3. This Norwegian archipelago in the Arctic Ocean is midway between continental Norway and the North Pole, and forms an unincorporated area administered by a state-appointed governor. ________

4. Two European countries share the barn swallow as their national bird. Name them. ________ and ________

5. Two European countries share the white stork as their national bird. Name them. ________ and __________

6. Four European countries share the oak as their national tree. Name them. ________, ________, ______ and ________

7. Three European countries share the olive as their national tree. Name them. _______, ______ and ________

8. Two European countries share the birch as their national tree. Name them. ________ and ______

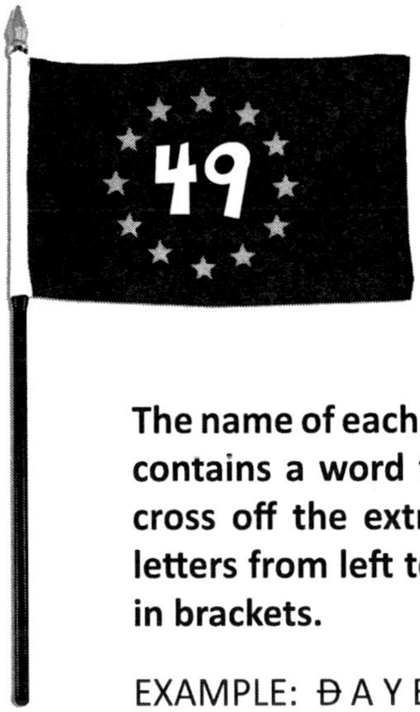

FOOD FOR THOUGHT

The name of each European traditional dish in the left hand column below contains a word that fits the clue given in that line. To find this word, cross off the extra letters in the food's name and read the remaining letters from left to right. The country to which this food belongs is given in brackets.

EXAMPLE: ~~D~~ A Y E ~~R~~ ~~E~~ ~~H~~ (Uzbekistan) How sailors say 'Yes' = AYE

	Food	Clue	Answer
1.	Kaiserschmarrn (Austria, shredded fluffy pancake)	Burn enough to blacken	________
2.	Æblekage (Denmark, apple charlotte)	You put things in it	________
3.	Soplillos (Spain, almond cakes)	Plants grow in it	________
4.	Saltibarsciai (Lithuania, cold beetroot soup)	They're in the night sky	________
5.	Caldo verde (Portugal, green kale soup)	A strong spice	________
6.	Maultaschen (Germany, Swabian ravioli)	A lot	________
7.	Lyutenitsa (Bulgaria, pepper relish)	You pitch them at camp	________
8.	Garnaalkroket (Belgium, shrimp croquette)	A tool to collect leaves	________
9.	Hangikjöt (Iceland, smoked lamb)	How you feel in the summer	________
10.	Chlodnik (Poland, cold beet soup)	A type of fish	________

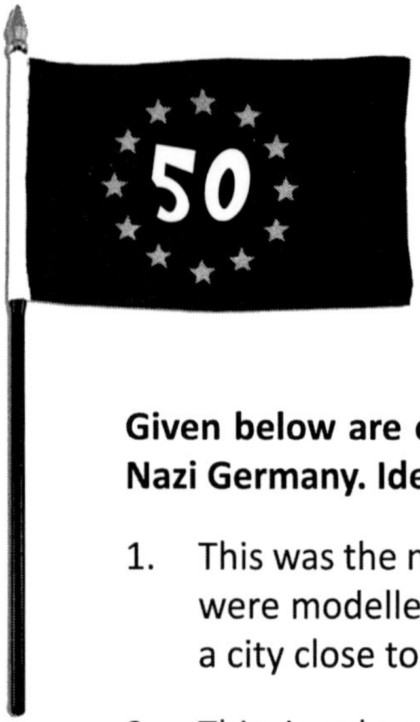

THE NAZI REGIME

Given below are clues to some of the places that gained importance in Nazi Germany. Identify the places by filling one letter in each blank.

1. This was the model concentration and death camp on which all others were modelled, located at a former World War I munitions factory, in a city close to Munich. _ _ _ _ _ _

2. This is where Hermann Goring announced the Race Laws which legalised the oppression of the Jews and severely curtailed their ability to participate in German public life. _ _ _ _ _ _ _ _ _

3. This is where the Nazi leadership gathered in 1942 to hammer out the Final Solution to the Jewish question. It was where the Holocaust began. _ _ _ _ _ _ _

4. The castle here was used by Heinrich Himmler, head of the SS, as a training ground for SS leaders. _ _ _ _ _ _ _ _ _ _

5. During the Cold War, this place was a key observation point right against the fortified border dividing East and West Germany. _ _ _ _ _ _ _ _ _ _

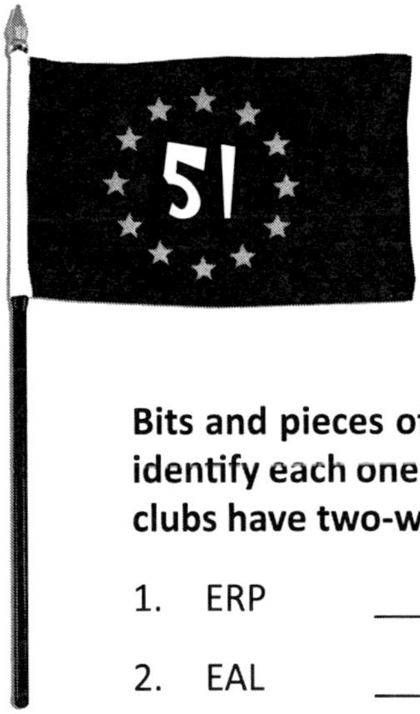

MID-GAME FRENZY

Bits and pieces of ten European football clubs are given below. Can you identify each one just by the letters that are given? Remember that some clubs have two-word names.

1. ERP ______________________
2. EAL ______________________
3. ELO ______________________
4. NIC ______________________
5. ANC ______________________
6. ENT ______________________
7. ILA ______________________
8. ELS ______________________
9. ONA ______________________
10. ENA ______________________

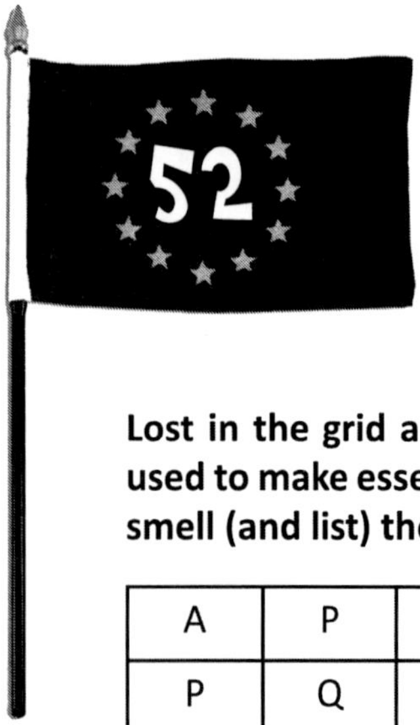

A SENSE OF SMELL

Lost in the grid are the names of ten aromatic plants grown in Europe used to make essential oils. Look diagonally, horizontally and vertically to smell (and list) them out. A letter may be used more than once.

A	P	R	A	J	E	S	T	L
P	Q	J	A	S	M	I	N	E
L	U	A	I	L	O	R	E	N
U	D	R	M	A	R	J	S	E
M	R	B	I	V	A	O	O	C
E	O	E	O	I	N	L	R	I
R	A	R	D	F	G	P	K	R
I	K	G	N	N	E	A	S	O
A	M	A	U	A	E	T	A	U
A	O	M	T	S	E	V	M	Q
L	S	O	M	I	T	Y	A	I
M	S	T	L	I	L	Y	D	L

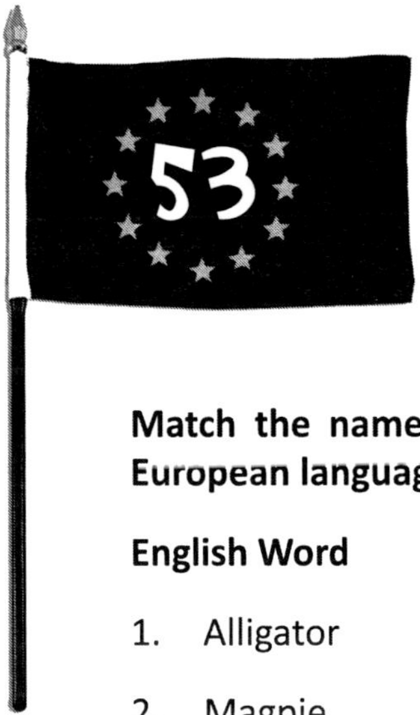

TRAVELLING WORDS

Match the names of the English words in the first column with the European language that inspired them.

English Word	European Language
1. Alligator	a. Italian
2. Magpie	b. Old Norse (Scandinavian)
3. Umbrella	c. Irish
4. Cookie	d. Czech
5. Wanderlust	e. Spanish
6. Sky	f. Swedish
7. Robot	g. Hungarian
8. Moped	h. Dutch
9. Paprika	i. French
10. Boycott	j. German

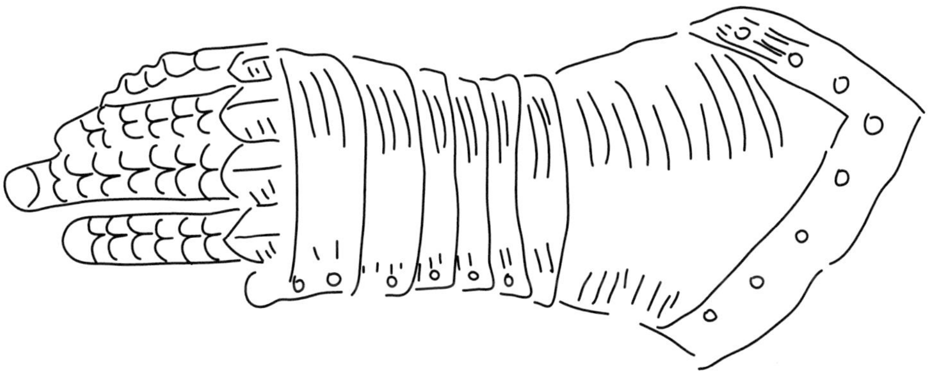

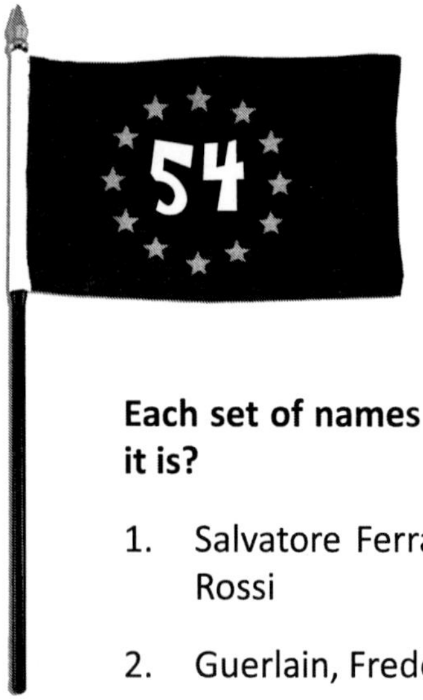

EUROPEAN LUXE

Each set of names below has something in common. Can you find what it is?

1. Salvatore Ferragamo, Christian Louboutin, Manolo Blahnik, Gianvito Rossi
2. Guerlain, Frederic Malle, Chanel, Cacharel
3. Dassault, Airbus, Lockheed Martin, Rolls-Royce
4. Patek Philippe, Breitling, Chopard, Piaget
5. Gucci, Louis Vuitton, Chanel, Prada
6. Aston Martin, Bentley, Bugatti, Rolls Royce
7. William Curley, Godiva, Pierre Marcolini, Charbonnel et Walker

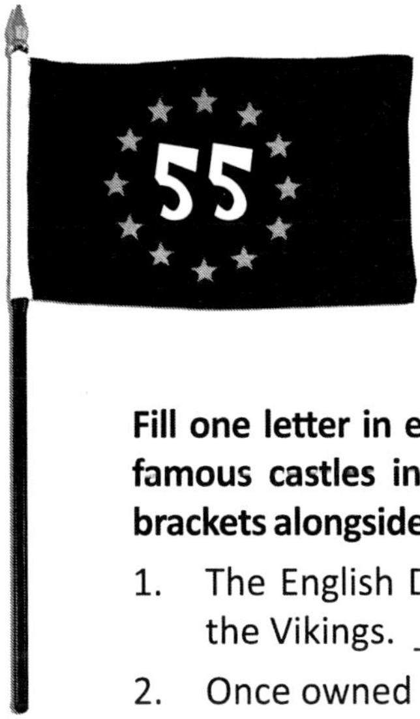

CASTLE-D

Fill one letter in each blank to solve the clue and find the names of some famous castles in Europe. The country to which they belong is given in brackets alongside major cities served by the train when it first began service.

1. The English Dukes of Hamilton built this castle as protection against the Vikings. _ _ _ _ _ _ _ _ (Scotland, United Kingdom)
2. Once owned by a noble family and a painter, this 12th century castle is now owned by the state and is a UNESCO World Heritage Site member, tourist site, museum and venue for cultural and leisure events. _ _ _ _ _ _ _ _ _ _ _ (Zagorje, Croatia)
3. Originally built in the 13th century by the Knights of the Teutonic Order, this castle has close ties to the legend of Dracula. _ _ _ _ (Romania)
4. Built on a rocky peak, this castle was originally an abbey. _ _ _ _ _ _ _ _-_ _ _ _ _ _ _ (France)
5. Henry Tudor was born in this castle situated on the banks of the River Estuary. _ _ _ _ _ _ _ _ _ (Wales, United Kingdom)
6. One of the largest castles in the world, it was built in the 9th century and stands majestic till today. _ _ _ _ _ _ (Czech Republic)
7. Built in the 11th century by Archbishop Gebhard, this massive fortress sits over a picturesque nearby town, and is one of the largest medieval castles in Europe. _ _ _ _ _ _ _ _ _ _ _ _ _ _ _ (Austria)
8. Situated in the hills between Koblenz and Trier, this well-preserved medieval castle has been owned by the same branch of the family for over 800 years. _ _ _ _ (Germany)
9. Destroyed and rebuilt many times over the years, this castle was once confiscated by the Nazis and then occupied by the Red Army. _ _ _ _ _ (Poland)
10. Built in the 15th century by the Archbishop, this castle is an excellent example of the Gothic and Mudejar styles. _ _ _ _ (Spain)

56

PLAY IT AGAIN

Given below are the names of famous classical Western music composers. Can you unscramble the letters given alongside each clue to find one of his most famous works?

1. Antonio Vivaldi. HET UROF ASNOSES _ _ _ _ _ _ _ _ _ _ _ _ _ _
2. Johann Sebastian Bach. BUNGRABDERN CROSTCONE _
3. George Frideric Handel. TREWA SCUMI _ _ _ _ _ _ _ _ _ _
4. Joseph Haydn. ETH INOTRACE _ _ _ _ _ _ _ _ _ _ _
5. Wolfgang Amadeus Mozart. EHT GRAMERIA FO FRAIGO _ _ _ _ _ _ _ _ _ _ _ _ _ _ _ _ _ _ _
6. Ludwig van Beethoven. TIFFH HYMNSYOP _ _ _ _ _ _ _ _ _ _ _ _ _ _
7. Franz Schubert. TREESIRINEW _ _ _ _ _ _ _ _ _ _ _ _
8. Johann Baptist Strauss. TRYZAKED CHARM _ _ _ _ _ _ _ _ _ _ _ _ _ _
9. Felix Mendelssohn. HET SHIREBED _ _ _ _ _ _ _ _ _ _ _
10. Frédéric Chopin. FLEARNU HARMC _ _ _ _ _ _ _ _ _ _ _ _
11. Richard Wagner. NILEHORNG _ _ _ _ _ _ _ _ _ _
12. Giuseppe Verdi. SAMES AD RIMEUEQ _ _ _ _ _ _ _ _ _ _ _ _ _ _
13. Pyotr Ilyich Tchaikovsky. ALVAUK ETH HISTM _ _ _ _ _ _ _ _ _ _ _ _ _ _
14. Sergei Rachmaninoff. RICACEP BINEHOME _ _ _ _ _ _ _ _ _ _ _ _ _ _ _
15. Béla Bartók. SHUSTOK _ _ _ _ _ _ _

ADVENTURES GALORE!

Join four letter groups from the box below to make the names of some characters who appear in the cartoon Tintin, by Herge. You have one clue for each character.

Cuth	Tarr	Son	Had	Doc	Ules
Nca	Tain	Bert	Teur	Casta	Ulus
Cap	Ras	Tap	Agon	Pson	Thom
Ler	Thom	Mul	Fiore	Calc	Ulos
	Herc	Bia	Dock	Opo	

1. The absent-minded inventor of genius.

    ____

2. The archetypal sailor, he often says, “Blistering barnacles!”.

    ____

3. Two blundering policemen who dress identically.
    __________________ and ________________

4. This vain opera singer is also called the Milanese nightingale.

    ____

5. This bad guy who is involved in the biggest crimes of the 20th century, he is often found in disguise. ______________________________

6. A specialist in American culture and history, and in the languages of the aboriginal inhabitants of America, he wears horn-rimmed glasses.

    ____

7. This Master of Evil first worked in the movie industry but then moved into narcotics and headed an occult organisation.

    ____

THE DRINK OF THE GODS

Arrange the names of the European wine-producing regions listed below into the grid. Once you are done, read the starred column top down to find the name of a prominent wine-growing region in France.

Alentejo (Portugal), Balaton (Hungary), Bardar (Moldova), Beresti (Romania), Caucasus (Russia), Chianti (Italy), Lemnos (Greece), Mosel (Germany), Rioja (Spain), Tikveš (Macedonia)

*

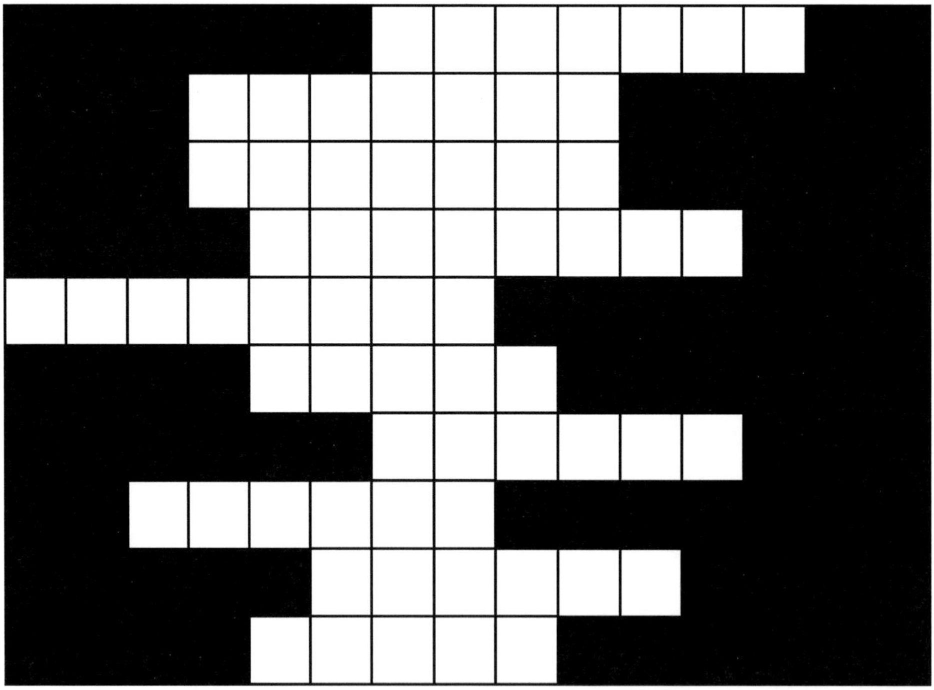

EAT YOUR VEGETABLES

Add the missing consonants to identify some vegetables that are native to Europe.

1. A _ _ I _ _ O _ E _
2. O _ I _ E _
3. _ U _ _ I _ _
4. _ A _ _ A _ E _
5. _ E _ E _ _
6. A _ _ A _ A _ U _
7. _ _ U _ _ E _   _ _ _ O U _ _
8. _ A _ _ _ I _ _
9. _ E _ _ U _ E
10. _ E E _ _ O O _

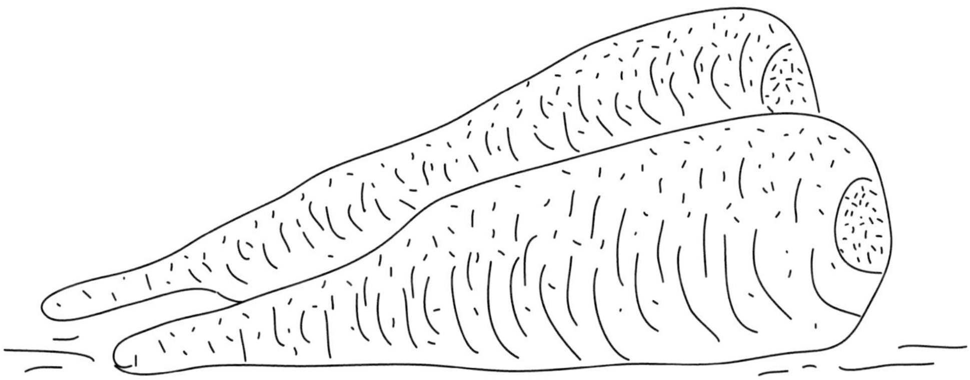

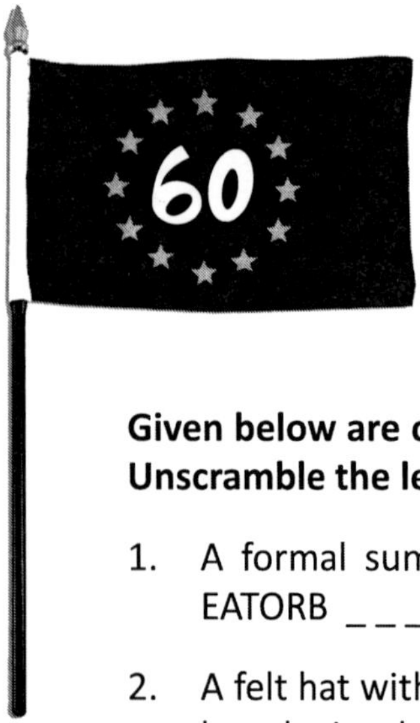

PUT A LID ON IT

Given below are clues to help you identify different types of men's hats. Unscramble the letters to find the answers.

1. A formal summer hat made of straw with a flat crown and brim. EATORB _ _ _ _ _ _
2. A felt hat with a wide brim and indented crown, it is typically creased lengthwise down the crown and pinched near the front on both sides. ADOREF _ _ _ _ _ _
3. Hats with a broad brim, three sides of which are turned up and either pinned, laced or buttoned in place to form a triangle around the crown. TERRINCO _ _ _ _ _ _ _ _
4. A formal felt hat characterised by a single dent running down the center of the crown, with a stiff brim shaped in a curl. HUGROMB _ _ _ _ _ _ _
5. A narrow-brimmed hat angled down at the front and slightly turned up at the back. BLYRIT _ _ _ _ _ _
6. A hard felt hat with a rounded crown. LOBREW _ _ _ _ _ _

A TOWERING EMPIRE

Can you arrange the Roman Emperors listed below in the order in which they reigned? Put numbers 1 to 10 against each blank, with 1 indicating the first emperor on the list, and 10 indicating the last.

Aurelian ______

Constantine II ______

Hadrian ______

Marcus Aurelius ______

Maximianus ______

Maximinus I ______

Nero ______

Septimius Severus ______

Tiberius ______

Vespasian ______

NOBEL WRITERS

Match the name of the winner of the Nobel Prize for Literature in Column A with the country to which s/he belongs in Column B, and one of the books for which s/he is known in Column C.

Nobel Prize Winner	Country	Book
1. Herta Müller	a. Sweden	i. Dora Bruder
2. Patrick Modiano	b. Italy	ii. The End and the Beginning
3. Elfriede Jelinek	c. Spain	iii. Accidental Death of an Anarchist
4. José Saramago	d. Poland	iv. Death of a Naturalist
5. Doris Lessing	e. Austria	v. The Family of Pascal Duarte
6. Tomas Tranströmer	f. Ireland	vi. The Piano Teacher
7. Wislawa Szymborska	g. Portugal	vii. The Land of Green Plums
8. Dario Fo	h. Germany	viii. The Good Terrorist
9. Seamus Heaney	i. France	ix. Blindness
10. Camilo Cela	j. Britain	x. For the Living and the Dead

HEADS UP!

Given below are the names of some European countries, with two names given against each. Tick the name of the person who <u>first</u> became head of government of the country.

1. Germany: Helmut Kohl / Angela Merkel
2. Greece: Antonis Samaras / George Papandreou
3. Portugal: António Guterres / Pedro Santana Lopes
4. Romania: Emil Boc / Adrian Năstase
5. Denmark: Anders Fogh Rasmussen / Lars Løkke Rasmussen
6. Russia: Viktor Alekseyevich Zubkov / Mikhail Yefimovich Fradkov
7. Belarus: Andrei Kobyakov / Mikhail Myasnikovich
8. Albania: Sali Berisha / Fatos Nano
9. Lithuania: Andrius Kubilius / Gediminas Kirkilas
10. Bulgaria: Sergei Stanishev / Plamen Oresharski
11. Iceland: Jóhanna Sigurðardóttir / Sigmundur Davíð Gunnlaugsson
12. Ireland: Bertie Ahern / Brian Cowen
13. Kosovo: Hashim Thaçi / Isa Mustafa
14. Andorra: Pere López Agràs / Jaume Bartumeu
15. Cyprus: Sibel Siber / İrsen Küçük

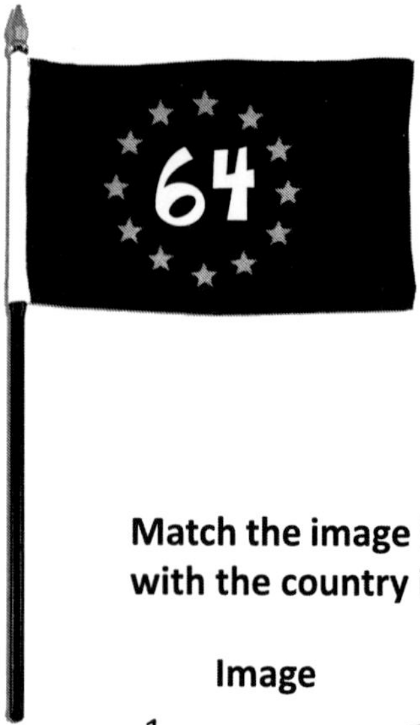

THE OLDEST OF THEM ALL

Match the image in Column A with the name of the building in Column B, with the country in which it is situated in Column C.

	Image	**Building**	**Country**
1.		a. Naveta d'Es Tudons, Spain	i. Most famous megalithic chamber tomb in Minorca
2.		b. Tumulus of Bougon, France	ii. A passage grave with one of the skulls showing the world's earliest dentistry work
3.		c. Hulbjerg Jaettestue, Denmark	iii. Oldest preserved stone house in northern Europe

4. 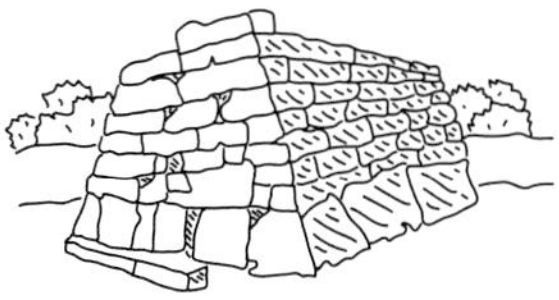 d. Tarxien, Malta iv. Minoan structure on a Neolithic site

5.  e. Knap of Howar, Scotland v. A group of five Neolithic barrows

6. 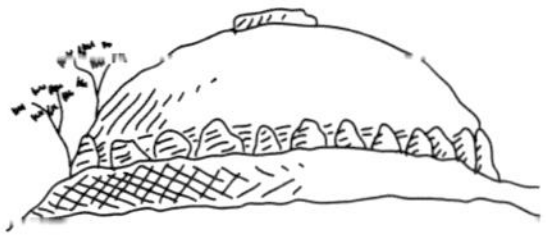 f. Knossos, Greece vi. A complex of tombs with varying dates

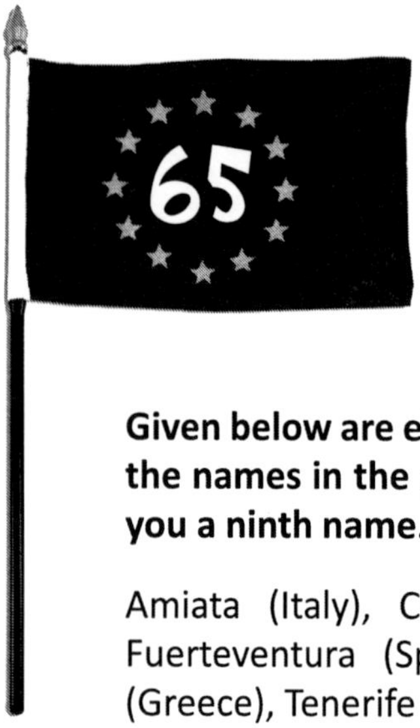

HIDDEN EXPLOSIVES

Given below are eight names which have something in common. Arrange the names in the grid so that reading down the starred column will give you a ninth name. Can you guess what is common to these nine names?

Amiata (Italy), Corvo (Azores, an autonomous region of Portugal), Fuerteventura (Spain), Kaiserstuhl (Germany), Kars (Turkey), Sousaki (Greece), Tenerife (Spain), Vulsini (Italy)

*

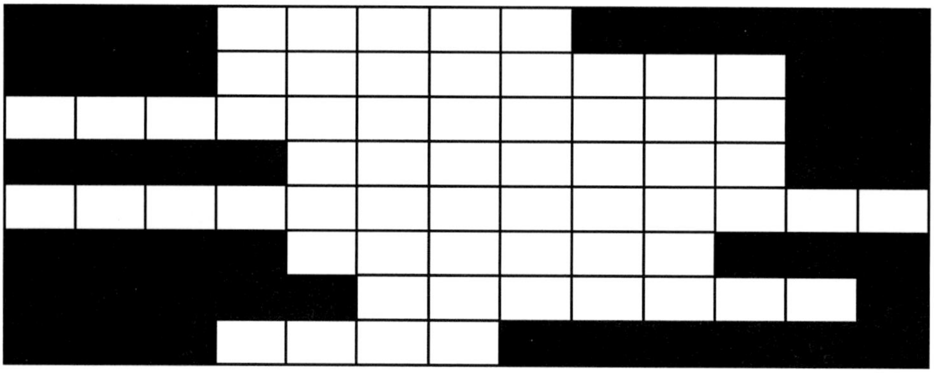

WHEN IN NETHERLANDS

Given below are clues to help you identify popular tourist attractions in Netherlands. Fill in the blanks to find the answer.

1. The world's largest flower garden, with tulips, hyacinths, daffodils and other spring flowers on display. _ _ _ _ _ _ _ _ _ _ GARDENS
2. Boasting of the oldest university in the Netherlands and beautiful canals, this city is the birthplace of Rembrandt. _ _ _ _ _ _
3. The largest concentration of over 1000 old Dutch windmills can be found near this village. _ _ _ _ _ _ _ _ _ _ _
4. This series of constructions has been created to protect large areas of land from the sea. _ _ _ _ _ _ _ _ _ _ _ _ _ _
5. This miniature park in The Hague features 1:25 scale model replicas of the most famous Dutch castles, industrial projects and public buildings. _ _ _ _ _ _ _ _ _ _
6. A fantasy-themed park, one of the oldest theme parks in the world, it has attractions spread over four fantastical realms: Fairy, Adventure, Travel and Alternative. _ _ _ _ _ _ _ _
7. A zoo that specialises in primates, it is the first park in the world where apes and monkeys are free to roam around the park amongst visitors. _ _ _ _ _ _ _ _
8. This is the location of the hiding place of the famed World War II diarist and her family during the German occupation of the Netherlands. _ _ _ _ _ _ _ _ _ HOUSE

PARK-ING JOYS

Choose one letter from the letters given below and fill it into a blank such that the word forms the name of the national park the clue describes. Each letter is used only once.

A B C D E F G H I J K L M

N O P Q R S T U V W X Y Z

1. Its shoreline is one of the wildest and most remote in England, and the extremely rare heath fritillary butterfly can be seen here where the forest borders the open spaces. E _ M O O _ (England)
2. This small park is covered by a thick laurel forest and nurtured by rich, volcanic soils. _ ARA _ O _ A _ (Spain)
3. It houses a remnant of the ancient forests (dating back 10,000 years) that once covered most of Europe, and animals such as the elk, the wild boar and the lynx that have disappeared across Europe thrive here. _ ELOVE _ _ SKAYA (Belarus)
4. The park includes a group of five picturesque villages perched high on the rocky Mediterranean coastline. _ IN _ UE _ ERR _ (Italy)
5. It began as a private foundation and houses a museum to showcase ways in which art and architecture can be in synchronicity with nature. H _ GE VELU _ E (Netherlands)
6. Germany's first national park, it is home to various uncommon bird species including Europe's smallest owl species, the pygmy owl. B _ VAR _ AN _ OREST NATIONAL PARK (Germany)

7. It is home to more than 70 glacial lakes, echoes of the last ice age. _ IRIN (Bulgaria)

8. It contains striking biodiversity despite being so close to the Arctic Circle because the limestone beneath the soil neutralises acids and helps provide the soil nutrients that boost plant growth. OU _ AN _ A NATIONAL PARK (Finland)

9. It is home to three breathtaking canyons, and includes Europe's deepest gorge. D _ R _ ITOR (Montenegro)

10. It is the only national park in France that has over 250 villages within its borders, making it a classic landscape of French traditional life. CÉ _ ENNE _ S (France)

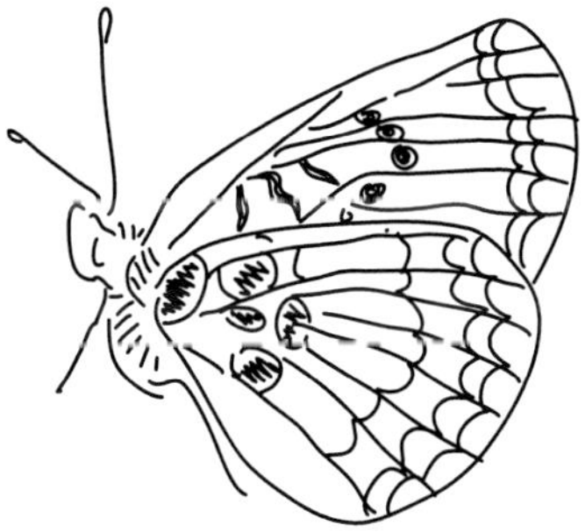

SPLIT PERSONALITIES

The letters of the names of two famous European sporting personalities have been mixed together in the correct order. The first two letters are the first letter in the name of each sportsperson. Separate the letters to find the two names. The sport they excel in, and the countries they are from are your clues.

1. R B O J G E O R R F N E B D E O R R E G R

   Tennis: Switzerland, Sweden

   Names: ______________________ and ______________________

2. S E E R M G Y L E Z I A B T U O B P E K K A

   Athletics: Soviet Union/Ukraine, Czechoslovakia (erstwhile)

   Names: ______________________ and ______________________

3. C D R A I V S I T D I B A E C N O K R O H N A L A D M O

   Football: Portugal, England

   Names: ______________________ and ______________________

4. M L I E C W H I S A H E A L M S I C L H U T M A O C N H E R

   Motor racing: Germany, Great Britain

   Names: ______________________ and ______________________

5. M J E A A R N I N I A E N L N O E N V G O O S

Cycling: Netherlands, France

Names: ________________________ and: ________________________

6. N S A V E D T L A I N A B O A G I N C S O K M A A N Y E C A I

Gymnastics: Romania, Soviet Union/Belarus

Names: ________________________ and: ________________________

7. A A N N N I N K A N A O S R O D Q R V E N I S A T S A T M

Golf: Sweden, Sweden

Names: ________________________ and: ________________________

8. A M A L R C B E E L H R I T R S O C T H O M E B R A

Skiing: Italy, Austria

Names: ________________________ and: ________________________

9. M G A A R G R N Y K U A S S P C A A R R L O S V E N

Chess: Norway, Russia

Names: ________________________ and: ________________________

10. C S A O N R J O L I A N H A K E O S N T I N E E R

Figure skating: Italy, Norway

Names: ________________________ and: ________________________

GAMES OF THE SMALL STATES OF EUROPE (GSSE)

Can you fill in these blanks correctly?

1. All nine members of the European small states have a population of less than 1 million except one country. Name this country. ____________________
2. The Games are held every _______________ years.
3. ______________________________ are also seeking to participate in the Games, but have not been allowed to do so.
4. The first ever edition of the Games was hosted by ____________________________ (city, country).
5. The first ever edition of the Games was hosted in the year _______________.
6. In 2015, the Games were held in ____________________.
7. The group began with eight members. Which country joined later?

POLITICAL STATEMENTS

Pick 3 words from the box (one for each blank) to correctly complete these quotes by prominent European politicians.

Socialist	Complete	Power	Lady	Truth	Democracy
Coat	Democracy	Soul	Statesmen	Observe	Mankind
Law	Politicians	Skin	Jesus	Political	Second
Freedom	Aren't	Language	Freedom	Power	Soul

1. ______________ is like being a ______________ ... if you have to tell people you are, you ______________. Margaret Thatcher

2. You start giving out your hat, then you give your ____________, then your shirt, then your ____________ and finally your ____________. Charles de Gaulle

3. ____________ was the first ____________, the first to seek a better life for ____________. Mikhail Gorbachev

4. If you must break the ____________, do it to seize ____________: in all other cases ____________ it. Julius Caesar

5. The world is weary of ____________ whom ____________ has degraded into ____________. Benjamin Disraeli

6. For us ____________ is a question of human dignity. And human dignity is ____________ ____________. Olof Palme

7. When a ____________ is not given complete freedom, ____________ is not ____________. Vaclav Havel

8. To have another ____________ is to possess a ____________ ____________. Charlemagne

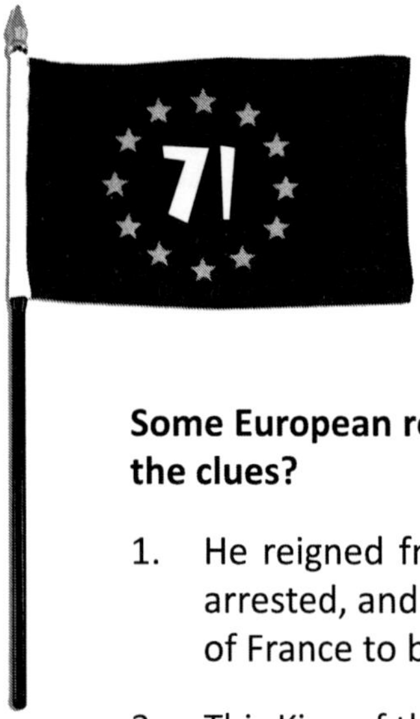

WHICH ROYAL AM I?

Some European royals are described below. Can you identify them using the clues?

1. He reigned from 1774 to 1792. He was found guilty of treason and arrested, and executed by the guillotine in 1793. He was the only King of France to be executed.

2. This King of the Belgians reigned for 44 years from 1865 to 1909, and is remembered mainly for the founding and exploitation of the Congo Free State and the subsequent genocide of millions of Congolese people.

3. He reigned over England and her dominions from 1910-1936, and in 1917, changed the family name from Saxe-Coburg-Gotha (popularly called Brunswick or Hanover) to Windsor, and relinquished all German titles and family connections.

4. She was queen regnant of Spain from 1833-1868. She came to the throne as an infant, but her succession was disputed by the Carlists who refused to recognise a female sovereign. She was deposed in 1868 and formally abdicated in 1870.

5. He was deeply hated in leftist circles because of his conservatism, and the anarchists attempted to assassinate him in the first year of his reign in 1878. In 1882 he approved the Triple Alliance with the German Empire and Austria-Hungary. His reign ended with his assassination in 1900 by another anarchist.

6. A Bavarian prince, he became the first modern King of Greece in 1832 under the Convention of London. He was unable to resolve Greece's poverty and economic meddling from outside powers throughout his reign. He was deposed in 1862 and died five years later in exile in Bavaria.

7. She was Queen regnant of Portugal from 1826-1828, and again from 1834-1853. Her father was the future King of Portugal and the First Emperor of Brazil, and she is the only European monarch to have been born outside Europe, though still in Portuguese territory. (She was born in Rio de Janeiro.) Her reign was notable for a public health act aimed at curbing the spread of cholera throughout the country.

8. He ruled as the last Holy Roman Emperor from 1792-1806, when he dissolved the Holy Roman Empire after his decisive defeat at the hands of Napoleon in the Battle of Austerlitz. He then founded the Austrian Empire and ruled as the first Emperor of Austria from 1804-1835, so he is named the only "Double Emperor" in history.

9. French by birth, he served a long career in the French Army, and was even appointed a Marshal of France by Napoleon. His service to France ended in 1810, when he was elected heir-presumptive to the Swedish throne because the Swedish royal family was dying out. On his ascension to the throne in 1818, he founded the House of Bernadotte, and reigned till 1844.

10. He was the King of Denmark from 1863-1906. Most of the years of his reign were dominated by political disputes, because Denmark had become a constitutional monarchy in 1849 and the balance of power between the sovereign and the parliament was still in dispute. His popularity recovered towards the end of his reign because of how long he ruled, and his high standards of personal morality.

11. The Emperor of Russia from 1825-1855, his reign was marked by geographical expansion, repression of dissent, economic stagnation, poor administrative policies, a corrupt bureaucracy and frequent wars that culminated in Russia's disastrous defeat in the Crimean War of 1853-56.

12. The last German Emperor (Kaiser) and King of Prussia. On being crowned in 1888, he dismissed the Chancellor of Germany, Otto von Bismarck in 1890 and launched Germany on a combative foreign policy that eventually culminated in the First World War. Bombastic and impetuous, he was an ineffective war leader and lost the support of the army, following which he abdicated in 1918 and fled to exile in the Netherlands.

FASHIONING THE PAST

Join two letter groups from the box below to make the names of some articles of clothing historically worn by men and women in Europe.

Aig	Fi	Ngale	Polo	Ple	Dle
Kin	Jab	Pann	Gir	Aloons	Chu
Oline	Wim	Farthi	Mers	Lande	Jer
Hen	Pant	Waist	Lets	Ot	Crin
Houppe	Bloo	lers	Nin	Naise	Shirt

1. A garment worn around the neck and chin which usually covers the head, this medieval headgear for women is still worn by some nuns.

   ____

2. Late in the 14th century, both men and women wore this robe with fullness falling from the shoulders, with wide trailing sleeves over their shirts and chemises. ______________________________

3. Women in the 15th century wore this cone or truncated cone-shaped cap with a wire frame covered in fabric and topped by a floating veil.

   ____

4. These hoop skirts were popular among noblewomen in Spain, England and France in the early 16th century. ______________________________

5. This sleeveless garment, usually made of leather, was often worn over the shirt and doublet by men in the late 16th century.

   ____

6. In the early 17th century, men wore hose or breeches fastened to doublets using ties with highly decorated metal tips called

   ______________________________.

7. Men wore this fabric fall at the throat, supported or attached by a neckband or collar; or simply pinned at the throat. ____________________

8. Women wore open-fronted bodices, with this lace or linen kerchief worn to fill in the low neckline. ____________________

9. Women's hoop skirts began to have side hoops, also called 'false hips' or ____________________.

10. Men began wearing these long tight breeches in the early 19th century. ____________________.

11. To achieve the narrow waist that was fashionable with the broad shoulders and wide, curvy hips, men began to wear the ____________________

12. This stiffened or structured petticoat was designed to hold out a woman's skirt from the mid-19th century onwards. ____________________

13. These loose trousers for women gathered at the ankles, topped by a short dress or skirt hemmed just below the knees, were introduced in the second half of the 19th century, though they did not become popular till much later. ____________________

14. This fitted, cutaway overdress skirt caught up and draped over an underskirt was popular among women in the late 19th century. ____________________

15. This women's costume had a bodice tailored like a man's shirt with a high collar, and was popular for informal daywear and became the uniform of working women in the early 20th century. ____________________

DANCING FOLK

Can you identify 15 European folk dances hidden in this grid? Find them diagonally, vertically and horizontally. A letter may be used more than once.

M	A	Z	U	R	K	A	Z	S	T
H	I	A	K	L	O	P	E	G	B
A	D	N	K	P	L	Q	N	N	H
S	R	Y	U	S	O	U	O	I	D
A	R	O	H	E	L	E	L	G	I
P	J	O	T	A	F	O	O	G	L
I	U	A	S	T	R	A	P	O	I
K	Q	U	A	D	R	I	L	L	E
O	G	N	A	D	N	A	F	C	C
K	A	R	T	U	L	I	S	E	T

BIRD IQ

Fill in each blank to make the name of a bird found in Europe. Then read down the blanks to find the name of the only city in Europe outside Greenland that starts with the letter Q, and the country to which it belongs.

COMMON _ UAIL (Ireland)

BLACK GRO _ SE (Slovakia)

LITTLE B _ TTERN (Bosnia & Herzegovina)

PYGMY _ ORMORANT (Albania)

SPOTTED CRA_ E (Malta)

WHIM _ REL (Faroe Islands)

BLUETHR _ AT (Estonia)

GREY PLOVE _ (Cyprus)

GARGA _ EY (Leichtenstein)

YELLOW WA _ TAIL (San Marino)

FEA'S PETR _ L (Britain)

_ UFF (Sweden)

_ ALLARD (Iceland)

ROCK PT _ RMIGAN (Andorra)

SAND MARTI _ (Finland)

EURASIAN JA _ (Austria)

ADIEU! ADIEU!

Unscramble the letters below to say goodbye in various European languages.

1. Spanish: ISODA _ _ _ _ _
2. French: ROVEAIRU _ _   _ _ _ _ _ _
3. Italian: CARDERIVEIRR _ _ _ _ _ _ _ _ _ _ _ _
4. Romanian: DARELEVEER _ _   _ _ _ _ _ _ _ _
5. German: FEWERAIDSHEENU _ _ _   _ _ _ _ _ _ _ _ _ _ _
6. Dutch: ZESTTION _ _ _   _ _ _ _ _
7. Swedish: JODA _ _ _ _
8. Danish: FLAVER _ _ _ _ _ _
9. Norwegian: HATEDBAR _ _   _ _ _   _ _ _
10. Polish: GAZENJ _ _ _ _ _ _

ANSWERS

1. Orient Express

1. Paris
2. Strasbourg
3. Munich
4. Vienna
5. Budapest
6. Bucharest
7. Istanbul

2. Delicious Shapes

1-f, 2-e, 3-i, 4-g, 5-j, 6-h, 7-a, 8-d, 9-c, 10-b

3. Arty Additions

1. Edgar Degas
2. Édouard Manet
3. Sandro Botticelli
4. El Greco
5. Peter Paul Rubens
6. Francisco de Goya
7. Paul Cézanne
8. Oscar-Claude Monet
9. Pierre Auguste Renoir
10. Paul Gauguin
11. Paul Klee
12. Diego Velázquez
13. Gustav Klimt
14. Marc Chagall
15. Joan Miró

4. Who Wrote It?

1. c. Cornelia Funke (Germany)
2. g. Jostein Gaarder (Norway)
3. i. Tove Jansson (Finland)
4. a. Eoin Colfer (Ireland)
5. j. Jean de Brunhoff (France)
6. b. Selma Lagerlof (Sweden)
7. e. Johanna Spyri (Switzerland)
8. f. Philip Pullman (Britain)
9. d. Carlos Ruiz Zafon (Spain)
10. h. Fabio Geda (Italy)

5. Say Cheese

1. ... magazine T"RICOT TA"lks about... (Ricotta, an Italian whey cheese)
2. ... be blanCHED, DARling. (Cheddar, a relatively hard, sharp-tasting cheese of England, U.K.)
3. The caFE TAble tops... (Feta, a crumbly aged curd cheese from Greece)
4. MauricE, DAMascus is not.... (Edam, a semi-hard cheese from the Netherlands)
5. ... new systEM, MEN TALly the liabilities... (Emmental, a yellow medium-hard cheese of Switzerland)
6. MarGO, UDAipur is the ... (Gouda, traditionally a Dutch yellow cheese made from cow's milk)
7. ... CaliBRI Edges out ... (Brie, a soft French cheese made of cow's milk)
8. GrandMA'S CARP ON English muffin... (Mascarpone, an Italian cheese made from cream)
9. SeesawS TILT ONe way and then... (Stilton, a semi-soft crumbly English cheese)
10. ... HarmoniCA MEMBER To pay their... (Camembert, a soft, creamy French cheese made of cow's milk)

6. A River Runs Through It

1. ... you sPOt five differences ... (PO, the longest river in Italy)
2. SteEL BEds are a... (ELBE, runs from the Czech Republic through Germany before flowing into the North Sea)
3. ... hear c"ODE R"ed, you should... (ODER, starts in the Czech Republic and flows through Poland and Germany)
4. ... GustaV, OLGA, and Nadia... (VOLGA, the longest river in Europe, viewed as the national river of Russia)
5. ... hearTH A MESs? (THAMES, the second-longest river in the United Kingdom)

6. ... of catarRH IN Every throat... (RHINE, flows through Switzerland, Germany and the Netherlands)
7. HelLO, IREne. It's... (LOIRE, the longest river in France)
8. ... can TAG US when you... (TAGUS, flows through Spain and Portugal before it empties into the Atlantic Ocean)
9. *DeaR, HONEy*, and... (RHONE, rises in Switzerland and flows through France into the Mediterranean Sea)
10. To be a SenSEI NEeds at least... (SEINE, it runs through Paris, the capital of France)

7. Peek-a-peak

Bard, Maze, Moss, Cord, Dean, Order, Snot, Base, Gross, Vandal.

8. Different Books, Common Theme

1-c, 2-e, 3-b, 4-f, 5-d, 6-a

All the novels are set in the time of the French Revolution.

9. Vowel Music

1. Bassoon
2. Trombone
3. Triangle
4. Oboe
5. Flute
6. Viola
7. Celesta
8. Glockenspiel
9. Marimba
10. Tuba

10. Revolutionary Facts

1-g, 2-e, 3-i, 4-h*, 5-j, 6-a*, 7-c, 8-f, 9-b, 10-d.

* Russia used the Julian calendar till February 1918, which differed slightly from the Gregorian calendar, which is still in use. The February Revolution (February according to the Julian Calendar) actually took place in March,

1917. The Bolshevik Revolution, also called the October Revolution took place in October, 1917 according to the Julian calendar, which was November in the Gregorian calendar.

11. Movie Magic

1-e,2-i, 3-j, 4-h, 5-g, 6-a, 7-d, 8-c, 9-b, 10-f

12. Counting Counties

						*				
G	J	I	R	O	K	A	S	T	E	R
					V	L	O	R	E	
				D	I	B	E	R		
			B	E	R	A	T			
E	L	B	A	S	A	N				
					F	I	E	R		
			T	I	R	A	N	A		

13. Dictating Terms

1. Napoleon Bonaparte. “Impossible is a word found only in the dictionary of fools.”
2. Adolf Hitler. “Words build bridges into unexplored regions.”
3. Benito Mussolini. “Better to live a day as a lion than a hundred years as a sheep.”

14. Intrepid Explorers

1. Vasco da Gama
2. Francisco Pizarro
3. Sir Francis Drake
4. Jacques Cartier
5. Hernando de Soto
6. Vasco Núñez de Balboa

15. Sir Winston Churchill Said...

G	R	S	U	C	C	E	S	S	A	P	R	T	A	R
A	C	O	N	S	I	S	T	S	T	O	O	F	R	M
G	O	I	N	G	D	R	F	R	O	M	P	T	A	E
I	F	A	I	L	U	R	E	S	T	R	O	T	T	O
D	R	U	M	B	O	F	A	I	L	U	R	E	S	E
A	W	I	T	H	O	U	T	Y	L	O	S	S	O	F
T	O	U	L	S	E	N	T	H	U	S	I	A	S	M

16. The Industrial Revolution

G	S	S	E	C	O	R	P	R	E	B	M	A	H	C	D	A	E	12 L	4 C
E	L	E	P	H	A	R	E	P	Q	R	S	T	A	M	M	A	T	R	O
R	18 T	H	R	E	S	H	I	N	G	M	A	C	H	I	N	E	B	L	T
M	I	L	E	E	N	I	H	C	A	M	G	N	I	L	L	I	8 M	C	T
17 S	E	E	D	D	R	I	L	L	D	L	B	A	E	V	L	T	Z	D	O
K	V	T	L	M	O	I	P	19 T	H	G	P	O	I	G	P	F	A	R	N
C	I	N	T	15 G	Y	E	N	M	R	7 L	13 B	L	E	A	C	H	I	N	G
Y	T	E	Y	A	G	N	L	5 S	A	O	P	S	A	T	O	L	U	11 S	I
P	O	M	R	S	S	O	N	T	F	A	N	R	T	T	T	G	M	T	N
H	M	E	I	L	E	R	H	E	T	A	R	P	E	N	E	O	S	E	E
I	O	C	G	I	G	E	N	A	J	U	S	O	L	F	A	9 M	N	A	M
Y	C	D	H	G	T	H	I	M	N	G	H	G	U	O	N	T	O	M	A
W	O	N	T	H	A	R	D	E	H	A	N	S	P	P	U	E	N	B	R
6 B	10 L	A	S	T	F	U	R	N	A	C	E	I	G	I	N	G	B	O	F
U	S	L	Q	I	T	W	E	G	C	A	N	N	N	N	O	T	H	A	R
G	L	T	U	N	U	A	R	I	A	N	T	E	E	N	I	B	L	T	E
W	O	R	I	G	H	A	T	N	W	I	L	L	H	A	I	Y	E	E	T
P	A	O	T	P	20 S	A	F	E	T	Y	L	A	M	P	S	R	L	D	A
E	N	14 P	16 C	Y	L	I	N	D	E	R	P	R	O	C	E	S	2 S	1 F	3 W
F	E	R	H	S	T	I	R	R	I	N	G	L	Y	P	O	E	T	I	C

17. Fashion A Designer

1. TEU V O LOMAN, Finland
2. HUSSEIN CHA L AYAN, Cyprus
3. PACO RA B ANNE, Spain
4. CATALIN BOTE Z ATU, Romania
5. BARBARA HULANIC K I, Poland
6. G INTS BUDE, Latvia
7. LUBICA KU C EROVA, Slovakia
8. HEL M UT LANG, Austria
9. D ARYL KERRIGAN, Ireland
10. AGNETA ECK E MYR, Sweden
11. GUNHILD N Y GAARD, Norway
12. ER T E, Russia
13. CHRISTIAN LACROI X, France
14. W ILBERT DAS, Netherlands
15. HUGO B O SS, Germany
16. JASPER CONR A N, Britain
17. ELENA VOT S I, Greece
18. P ETER JENSEN, Denmark
19. ZIKA ASC H ER, Czech Republic
20. F ELIPE OLIVEIRA BAPTISTA, Portugal
21. FRANCO MOSCHI N O, Italy
22. D R IES VAN NOTEN, Belgium
23. KATERENA DEPAS Q UALE, Ukraine
24. ETIENNE A I GNER, Hungary
25. JEAN-CHARLES DE CASTELBA J AC, Morocco
26. ROBERT PIG U ET, Switzerland

18. Feathered Symbols

1. Croatia – Nightingale
2. Romania – Great white pelican
3. Lithuania – White stork
4. Luxembourg – Goldcrest
5. Estonia – Barn swallow
6. Italy – Golden eagle
7. Germany – White-tailed eagle
8. Russia – Tundra swan
9. United Kingdom – European robin
10. Greece – Little owl

19. Who Art Thou?

Portia, Montague, Imogen, Bertram, Malcolm, Desdemona, Gertrude, Shylock, Petruchio, Hermia

20. Hiding From Danger

1. Roach's mouse-tailed dormouse
2. North Atlantic right whale
5. Corsican hare
4. Madeira pipistrelle
5. Canary long-eared bat
6. Bavarian pine vole
7. Iberian lynx
8. Saiga antelope
9. European mink
10. Azorean bat
11. Sandy mole rat
12. Canary shrew
13. Slender-billed curlew
14. Karpathos frog
15. Apennine chamois
16. Montseny brook newt
17. Batuecan rock lizard
18. Aegean Minnow
19. Carabo Beetle
20. Azores Bullfinch

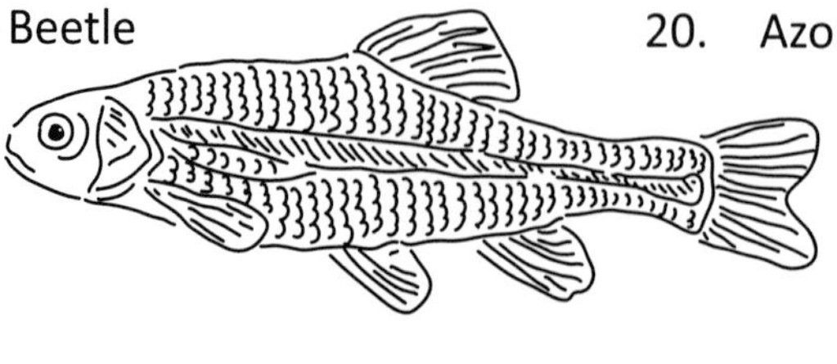

1 R	F	G	T	R	N	M	B	Q	T	P	E	L	M	A	N	I	S	M	A	B	E	C	L	P
2 N	O	R	T	H	A	T	L	A	N	T	I	C	R	I	G	H	T	W	H	A	L	E	R	S
V	B	A	N	L	Z	H	B	Q	F	P	A	D	M	N	F	T	Y	A	E	W	L	M	T	B
T	S	R	C	G	A	N	C	U	M	N	B	E	L	T	E	D	S	O	N	G	E	O	J	A
X	D	U	R	H	A	E	Z	N	A	V	E	R	B	O	T	E	B	B	E	S	R	N	K	V
N	D	D	E	E	S	C	R	R	I	E	C	E	R	T	I	B	N	H	E	S	T	T	W	A
Y	R	R	R	W	E	M	Y	Q	L	F	G	A	Y	B	Y	S	M	U	N	G	S	S	E	R
L	A	O	N	C	T	S	O	T	P	A	L	E	R	G	E	N	T	S	E	B		E	L	I
N	Z	S	U	A	H	A	J	U	R	O	O	L	A	L	A	M	B	O	U	R	P	N	R	A
A	I	U	R	R	A	I	U	E	S	M	M	G	U	N	S	T	A	M	E	N		Y	U	N
	L	M	E	A	V	G	M	Q	S	E	S	N	R	B	M	F	L	I	X	E	P	B	C	P
R	K	W	I	B	B	A	B	M	T	T	T	D	E	R	S	I	F	T	Z	B	A	R	D	I
E	C	U	F	O	N	A	L	I	R	A	L	A	C	R	S	E	N	L	A	S	R	O	E	N
B	O	J	E	B	U	N	E	R	I	R	L	M	I	S	A	A	R	N	T	S		O	L	E
I	R	M	L	E	J	T	V	B	N	E	I	E	R	L	O	H	U	O	O	Q	E	K	L	V
M	N	U	T	E	K	E	E	S	G	L	B	L	U	W	E	Y	N	O	Z	W	D	N		O
A	A	Y	B	T	U	L	R	U	Y	O	C	L	M	Y	E	D	O	A	S	A	A	E	B	L
R	C	H	I	I	F	O	T	M	P	M	I	O	B	L	I	U	D	N	C	R	M	W	R	E
B	E	B	R	E	S	P	E	T	L	Y	T	W	I	E	R	C	H	O	I	I	E	T	E	I
I	U	O	C	A	S	E	X	I	O	D	N	D	Z	R	D	A	N	T	R	E	S	L	D	T
O	T	K	H	A	E	F	C	L	Y	N	A	Y	A	R	F	O	R	E	V	M	N	R	N	E
N	A	S	C	D	G	S	I	O	M	A	H	C	E	N	I	N	N	E	P	A	O	E	O	Y
T	B	F	I	G	U	N	E	T	F	S	R	S	L	O	P	M	Z	A	S	E	B	U	L	C
C	A	N	A	R	Y	L	O	N	G	E	A	R	E	D	B	A	T	C	R	A	F	T	S	Y
T	G	O	R	F	S	O	H	T	A	P	R	A	K	N	I	M	N	A	E	P	O	R	U	E

21. What Are You Saying?

1-g, 2-e, 3-i, 4-j, 5-d, 6-a, 7-m, 8-f, 9-n, 10-c, 11-l, 12-o, 13-k, 14-b, 15-h

22. Famous Titles

[1]T	H	E	[2]D	I	V	I	N	E	C	O	M	E	D	Y						
H			O																	
E			N		[3]T	H	E	M	E	T	A	M	O	R	P	H	O	S	I	S
M			Q																	
A		[4]J	U	D	E	T	H	E	O	B	S	C	U	R	E		[5]M		[6]W	
S			I														R		I	
T			X				[7]F	A	T	H	E	R	S	A	N	D	S	O	N	S
E			O		[8]E		A										D		N	
R			T		M		U		[9]D								A		I	
A		[10]L	E	S	M	I	S	E	R	A	B	L	E	S			L		E	
N					A		T		A								L		T	
D									C								O		H	
M					[11]T	A	R	T	U	F	F	E			[12]M		W		E	
A		[13]C							L						A		A		P	
R		A							A						C		Y		O	
G		N													B				O	
A		[14]D	A	V	I	D	C	O	P	P	E	R	F	I	E	L	D		H	
R		I													T					
I		D													H					
[15]T	H	E	S	E	C	R	E	T	G	A	R	D	E	N						
A																				

23. Fairytale Confusion

1. Beanstalk
2. Breadcrumbs
3. Pea
4. Slipper
5. A kiss
6. Apple
7. Eyes

8. Hair
9. Porridge
10. Rats
11. Lied
12. Wolf

24. Rhyme Riddles

1-d, 2-e, 3-f, 4-a, 5-c, 6-b

1. **Ring a ring of roses** refers to the Great Plague of London in 1665, which caused a high fever and a rash in the form of a ring. Herbs and spices were put in the pockets of ailing people to freshen up the stale air, giving rise to the term "pocket full of posies".
2. **Here we go round the mulberry bush** refers to the 420-year-old Wakefield Prison's female prisoners, who exercised around a mulberry tree.
3. **Mary, Mary, quite contrary** refers to Mary I, daughter of Henry VIII, who executed Protestant loyalists. Silver bells and cockleshells were the instruments of torture at the time.
4. **Baa, baa, black sheep**: In the 13th century, King Edward I imposed a tax on wool so that one-third the price of a sack of wool went to the king, another third to the church, and the remaining one-third to the farmer, with no money left over for the shepherd boy.
5. **Three blind mice** are the three Protestant loyalists accused of plotting against Queen Mary I. The queen owned many large estates with her husband, King Philip of Spain, and is referred to as the farmer's wife. The three men were burned at the stake.
6. **Humpty Dumpty** refers to the cannon used to gain control over the city of Colchester during the English Civil War, after which the cannon sat on a church tower until cannonballs destroyed the tower, and the cannon fell into the marshland below.

25. Adding Up Science

1. Wilhelm Conrad RÖNTGEN
2. Evangelista TORRICELLI
3. ARISTOTLE
4. Levi STRAUSS
5. Amalie Auguste Melitta BENTZ
6. Guglielmo MARCONI
7. Marie CURIE
8. John Logie BAIRD
9. Alexander FLEMING
10. Claude-Étienne MINIÉ
11. Carl Wilhelm SCHEELE
12. Edmund CARTWRIGHT
13. Antoine Laurent LAVOISIER
14. Zacharis JANSSEN
15. Michael FARADAY

26. Find The Common Thread

11 B	E	L	U	S	H	Y	A	G	U	B	A
T	G	A	V	S	G	N	I	N	N	O	H 12
S	U 3	13 U	U	M	M	A	N	N	A	Q	T
E	P	H	T	5 M	A	E	Y	A	R	E	A
F	E	Q 2	U	U	G	N	O	S	K	I	D 9
R	R	A	I	R	6 N	O	R	I	L	S	K
E	N	A	M	M	A	7 T	R	O	M	S	O
M	A	N	I	A	T	B	O	V	E	T	H
M	V	A	S	N	A	E	A	R	C	T	I
A	I	A	I	S	H	C	10 T	I	K	S	I
14 H	K	Q	S 8	K	K 4	C	I	R	C	L	E
N	E	Y	B	R	A	E	Y	G	N	O	L 1

They are above the Arctic Circle.

27. Sightseeing

1. Trevi Fountain
2. Arc de Triomphe
3. Stonehenge
4. Eiffel Tower
5. Leaning Tower
6. La Sagrada Familia
7. Tower of London
8. Parthenon
9. Brandenburg Gate
10. Colosseum

28. Fording The Fjords

1. Bile
2. Chive
3. Orbs
4. Labour
5. Lab
6. Four
7. Light
8. Bus
9. Ginger
10. Ears

29. Who Solved It?

1. Jules Maigret
2. Kurt Wallander
3. Mikael Blomkvist
4. Peter Wimsey
5. Gervase Fen
6. Father Brown
7. John Rebus

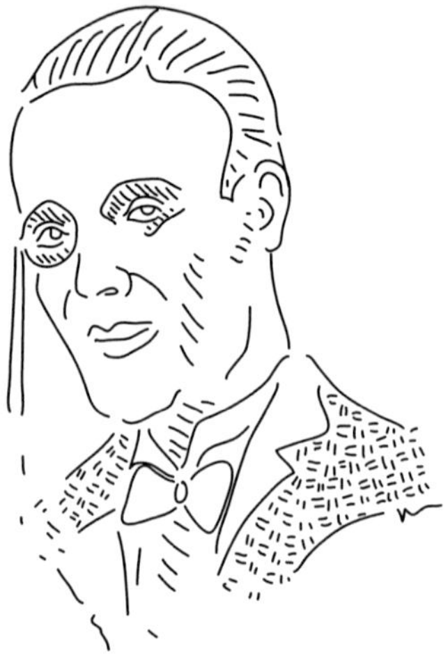

8. Pepe Carvalho
9. Adam Dalgliesh
10. Salvo Montalbano

30. Did You Know?

1. Denmark
2. Iceland's capital Reykjavik is the northern-most capital of a sovereign state.
3. Vatican City
4. Malta—the language is Maltese.
5. Denmark's flag dates from the second half of the 14th century.
6. San Marino, located on Mt Titano in north-central Italy.
7. Andorra
8. Principality of Monaco, with over 17,700 people per square km in 2010 and an unemployment rate of 0% in 2010 according to World Bank data.
9. Malta—the inhabited islands are Malta, Gozo and Comino.
10. Liechtenstein

31. Gods With Jobs

Roman:

Minerva – Goddess of Wisdom

Saturn – God of Time

Neptune – God of the Sea

Apollo – God of the Sun (Apollo is both a Roman and a Greek God. He is also considered the God of Music, Poetry, Art, Medicine, Archery etc.)

Bacchus – God of Wine

Greek:

Aphrodite – Goddess of Love

Hephaestus – God of Fire

Demeter – Goddess of Grain

Hermes – God of Travel

Artemis – Goddess of the Hunt

32. Norse Mythology

Apple, Starfruit, Guava, Apricot, Raisins, Dates – ASGARD, where the gods lived

Mango, Ivy gourd, Durian, Grapes, Avocado, Raspberry, Drumstick – MIDGARD, the world of men

Nectarine, Iceberg Lettuce, Fig, Lychee, Horseradish, Eggplant, Indian pea, Musk melon – NIFLHEIM, the world of the dead

33. Main Bits

1. PRAGUE, Czech Republic
2. RIGA, Latvia
3. VALLETTA, Malta
4. CHISINAU, Moldova
5. BUCHAREST, Romania
6. BRATISLAVA, Slovakia
7. ATHENS, Greece
8. COPENHAGEN, Denmark
9. MOSCOW, Russia
10. PODGORICA, Montenegro
11. TIRANA, Albania
12. MADRID, Spain

13. TALLINN, Estonia
14. PARIS, France
15. BUDAPEST, Hungary

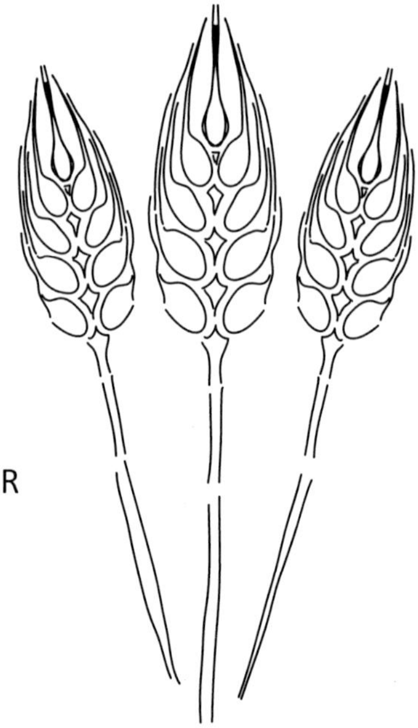

34. From Here to There

CORK – CORN – COON – SOON – SION

PORI – PORK – PERK – PEAK – PEAR – HEAR – HVAR

SALO – SALT – MALT – MAST – MOST

35. Changing City Names

1. Zagreb, Agram – Croatia
2. Nuuk, Godthaab – Greenland
3. Tallinn, Revel – Estonia
4. Strasbourg, Argentoratum – France
5. Paris, Lutetia – France
6. Bologna, Felsina – Italy
7. Podgorica, Titograd - Montenegro
8. Maastricht, Traiectum – Netherlands
9. Gdansk, Danzig – Poland
10. Saint Petersburg, Petrograd – Russia
11. Uppsala, Ostra Aros – Sweden
12. Odessa, Hacibey – Ukraine
13. Yekaterinburg, Sverdlovsk – Russia
14. Brasov, Kronstadt – Romania
15. Lisbon, Olisipo - Portugal

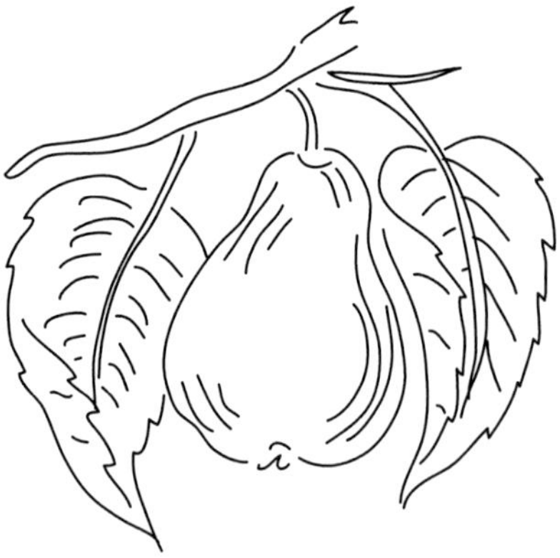

36. Gypsy Rhythms

APAAH	AFBRAS	MIAR ARU	CR I R E E AT
S INTI	BOYASH	E RLI DE S	ROMUNG RO
HNDED	S R EGKE	TE LMODE	YD P E DO TE

37. A-MAZE-ing Scripts

1 9 I	3 L	E	6 M	I	S	2 H	U	N	14 G	A	R	I	A	N 8
I	I	B	A	T	D	S	P	10 R	F	R	V	A	O	A
N	T	G	C	U	S	I	K	O	13 P	G	E	R	F	M
N	H	C	E	Z	C 4	D	E	M	K	O	W	E	H	R
I	U	D	D	20 I	M	E	S	A	P	E	L	C	K	E
S	A	Y	O	T	X	W	C	N	G	I	T	I	L	15 G
H	N	N	N	A	N	5 S	Z	I	D	U	B	D	S 17	O
S	I	A	I	L	C	R	A	A	11 D	T	J	N	E	H
I	A	I	A	I	W	N	P	N	A	Q	U	A	R	S
N	N	V	N	A	I	T	A	O	R	19 C	T	L	B	I
A	H	U	R	N	A	I	S	S	U	23 R	I	E	I	L
P	C	D	E	F	L	O	I	P	B	T	H	C	A	G
22 S	T	L	24 S	L	O	V	E	N	I	A	N	12 I	N	N
P	U	O	S	T	I	N	N	A	I	N	O	T	S	18 16 E
I	D	7 M	A	M	B	N	A	I	N	I	A	R	K	U 21

38. Starry Fame

1. Ingrid Bergman
2. Sophia Loren
3. Vivien Leigh
4. Brigitte Bardot
5. Judi Dench
6. Julie Christie
7. Maureen O’Hara
8. Audrey Hepburn
9. Romy Schneider
10. Barbara Sukowa

39. Double Date Trouble

1. 753 BC
2. 1492
3. 1792
4. 1922
5. 1994
6. 1498
7. 1993
8. 1989
9. 1986
10. 1999

40. Red, White and Blue

1. Croatia
2. Luxembourg
3. Russia
4. Norway
5. United Kingdom
6. Slovenia
7. France
8. Iceland
9. Netherlands
10. Serbia

41. Now You See It, Now You Don't!

1. verMIN SKate – MINSK, Belarus
2. ilyiCH IS IN AUstria – CHISINAU, Moldova
3. avanTI RAN Away – TIRANA, Albania
4. micawBER LINgered – BERLIN, Germany
5. giVE NICE – VENICE, Italy
6. GENE VAriations – GENEVA, Switzerland
7. MarCO LOG NEarly – COLOGNE, Germany

8. SlowLY ON – LYON, France
9. SometimeS EVIL LEaves – SEVILLE, Spain
10. WomBAT Has – BATH, United Kingdom
11. ailinG HEN Thrashed – GHENT, Belgium
12. acknowledGE NOAh's – GENOA, Italy
13. NimMO SCOWled – MOSCOW, Russia
14. CarouseL IS BONded – LISBON, Portugal
15. AhMAD RID – MADRID, Spain

42. The European Union

A	I	N	A	M	O	R [9]	D [3]	A	I	V	T	A	L [1]
L	C	Z	E	C	H	R	E	P	U	B	L	I	C
G	E	R	M	A	N	Y	N	[5] E	C	E	E	R	G [4]
E	I	N	C	H	T	E	M	[13] S	W	E	D	E	N
N	A	I	R	T	S	U	A [10]	T	S	T	E	I	N
D	N	A	L	N	I	F [12]	R	O	[15] M	A	L	T	A
R	U	P	S	S	I	A	K	N	Y	L	A	T	I [14]
N	O	[11] S [7]	L	O	V	E	N	I	A	R	W	A	Y
S	E	[8] P	O	R	T	U	G	A	L	R	B	I	A

The member countries of the European Union are: Latvia, Czech Republic, Denmark, Greece, Estonia, Germany, Spain, Portugal, Romania, Austria, Slovenia, Finland, Sweden, Italy, Malta

The non-member countries of the European Union are: Leichtenstein, Russia, Norway, Serbia

43. Porter

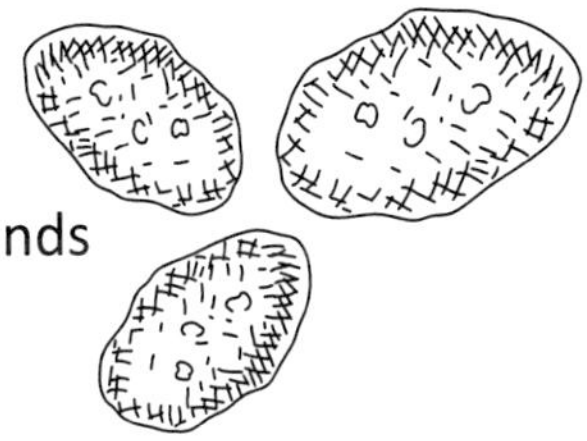

1. Le Havre, France
2. Piraeus, Greece
3. Dublin, Ireland
4. Rotterdam, Netherlands
5. Antwerp, Belgium
6. Algeciras, Spain

7. Bremerhaven, Germany
8. La Spezia, Italy
9. Felixstowe, United Kingdom
10. Marsaxlokk, Malta

44. A Vegetable By Another Name

Potato.

45. How Green Is My Land!

Kayak, After, Lift, Alter, Anger, Limb, Light, Ink, Stain, Under, Train - KALAALLISUT

Trunk, Urban, Never, Ulster, Miser, Inner, Irate, Stun, Ukelele, Trash - TUNUMIISUT

Image, Noble, Uniform, Knit, Tempo, Unity, Narrow - INUKTUN

46. It's Complicated

					*					
					F	A	M	J	I	N
V	E	S	T	M	A	N	N	A		
	H	U	S	A	R					
				H	O	V				
					E	I	O	I		
R	U	N	A	V	I	K				
			N	E	S					
		H	V	A	L	B	A			
T	O	R	S	H	A	V	N			
			K	U	N	O	Y			
		S	A	N	D	U	R			
					S	U	M	B	A	

Faroe Islands. Between 1035 and 1814, the Faroe Islands were part of the Kingdom of Norway. The 1814 Treaty of Kiel granted Denmark control over the islands, along with two other Norwegian regions, Greenland and Iceland. The Faroe Islands have been a self-governing country within the Danish Realm since 1948. The Faroese have control of most domestic matters; areas that remain the responsibility of Denmark include military defence, police, justice, currency and foreign affairs. The Faroe Islands have representation in the Nordic Council as members of the Danish delegation.

47. Mixed-Up Waters

1. North and Aegean Seas
2. Ionian and Barents Seas
3. Ligurian and Baltic Seas
4. Irish and Adriatic Seas
5. White and Norwegian Seas

48. National Tidbits

1. Netherlands. Its flag is red, white and blue, but the national colour is orange.
2. Germany and Austria
3. Svalbard
4. Austria and Estonia
5. Belarus and Lithuania
6. Estonia, Germany, Italy and Moldova
7. Greece, Italy and Albania
8. Finland and Russia

49. Food For Thought

1. Char
2. Bag
3. Soil
4. Stars
5. Clove
6. Much
7. Tents
8. Rake
9. Hot
10. Cod

50. The Nazi Regime

1. Dachau
2. Nuremberg
3. Wannsee
4. Wewelsburg
5. Point Alpha

51. Mid-game Frenzy

1. LivERPool
2. REAL Madrid
3. BarcELOna
4. Bayern MuNICh
5. MANChester United
6. JuvENTus
7. MILAn
8. ChELSea
9. InternaziONAle
10. ArsENAl

52. A Sense Of Smell

A	P	R	A	J	E	S	T	L
P 7	Q	10 J	A	S	M	I	N	E
L	U	A	I	L	O 3	R	E	N 8
U	D	R	M	A	R	J	S	E
M	R	B	I	V	A	O	O	C
E	6 O	E	O	I	N	L	R	I
R	A	R	D	F	G	P	K	R
I	K	G	N	N	E	A	S	O
A	M	A	U	A	E	T	A	U
A	O	M	T	S	E	V	M	Q
L	S	O	M	I	T	Y	A	I
M	S	T	5 L	I	L	Y	9 D	4 L 1

53. Travelling Words

1-e, 2-i, 3-a, 4-h, 5-j, 6-b, 7-d, 8-f, 9-g, 10-c

54. European Luxe

They are all:

1. Shoes
2. Perfumes
3. Airplane manufacturers
4. Watches
5. Leather goods
6. Cars
7. Chocolates

55. Castle-d

1. Brodick Castle, United Kingdom
2. Veliki Tabor Castle, Croatia
3. Bran Castle, Romania
4. Mont Saint-Michel, France
5. Pembroke Castle, Wales, United Kingdom
6. Prague Castle, Czech Republic
7. Hohensalzburg Castle, Austria
8. Eltz Castle, Germany
9. Ksiaz Castle, Poland
10. Coca Castle, Segovia, Spain

56. Play It Again

1. The Four Seasons
2. Brandenburg Concertos
3. Water Music
4. The Creation
5. The Marriage of Figaro
6. Fifth Symphony
7. Winterreise
8. Radetzky March
9. The Hebrides
10. Funeral March
11. Lohengrin
12. Messa da Requiem
13. Vakula the Smith
14. Caprice Bohemien
15. Kossuth

57. Adventures Galore!

1. Cuthbert Calculus
2. Captain Haddock
3. Thompson and Thomson
4. Bianca Castafiore
5. Docteur Muller
6. Hercules Tarragon
7. Rastapopoulos

58. The Drink of the Gods

						*						
						B	A	L	A	T	O	N
			B	E	R	E	S	T	I			
			C	H	I	A	N	T	I			
				C	A	U	C	A	S	U	S	
A	L	E	N	T	E	J	O					
				R	I	O	J	A				
						L	E	M	N	O	S	
		B	A	R	D	A	R					
					T	I	K	V	E	S		
				M	O	S	E	L				

Beaujolais.

59. Eat Your Vegetables

1. Artichokes
2. Olives
3. Turnips
4. Cabbages
5. Celery
6. Asparagus
7. Brussel Sprouts
8. Parsnips
9. Lettuce
10. Beetroot

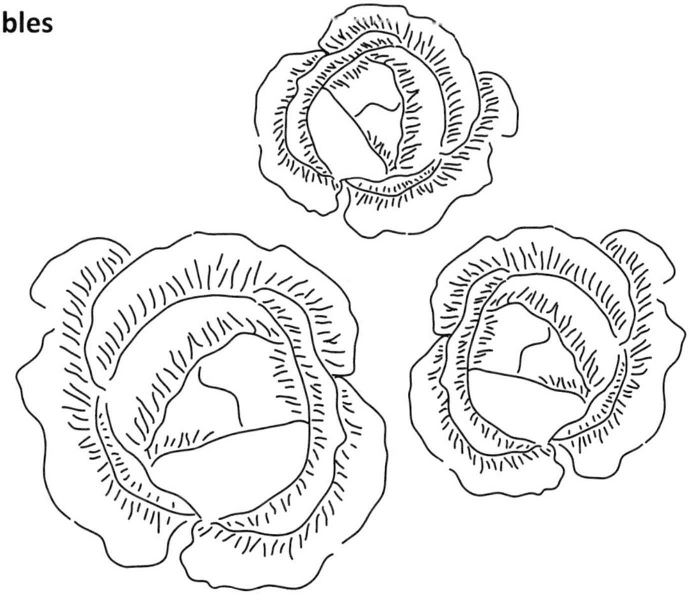

60. Put A Lid On It

1. Boater
2. Fedora
3. Tricorne
4. Homburg
5. Trilby
6. Bowler

61. A Towering Empire

1. Tiberius	(14-37 AD)
2. Nero	(54-68 AD)
3. Vespasian	(69-79 AD)
4. Hadrian	(117-138 AD)
5. Marcus Aurelius	(161-180 AD)
6. Septimius Severus	(193-211 AD)
7. Maximinus I	(235-238 AD)
8. Aurelian	(270-275 AD)
9. Maximianus	(286-305 AD)
10. Constantine II	(337-340 AD)

62. Nobel Writers

1. Herta Muller – h. Germany – vii. The Land of Green Plums
2. Patrick Modiano – i. France – i. Dora Bruder
3. Elfriede Jelinek – e. Austria – vi. The Piano Teacher
4. Jose Saramago – g. Portugal – ix. Blindness
5. Doris Lessing – j. Britain – viii. The Good Terrorist

6. Tomas Transtroemer – a. Sweden – x. For the Living and the Dead
7. Wislawa Szymborska – d. Poland – ii. The End and the Beginning
8. Dario Fo – b. Italy – iii. Accidental Death of an Anarchist
9. Seamus Heaney – f. Ireland – iv. Death of a Naturalist
10. Camilo Cela – c. Spain – v. The Family of Pascual Duarte

63. Heads Up!

1. Helmut Kohl (1982-1998)
2. George Papandreou (2009-2011)
3. Antonio Guterres (1995-2002)
4. Adrian Nastase (2000-2004)
5. Anders Fogh Rasmussen (2001-2009)
6. Mikhail Yefimovich Fradkov (2004-2007)
7. Mikhail Myasnikovich (2010-2014)
8. Fatos Nano (2002-2005)
9. Gediminas Kirkilas (2006-2008)
10. Sergei Stanishev (2005-2009)
11. Johanna Siguroardottir (2009-2013)
12. Bertie Ahern (1997-2008)
13. Hashim Thaci (2008-2014)
14. Jaume Bartumeu (2009-2011)
15. Irsen Kucuk (2010-2013)

64. The Oldest Of Them All

1-f-iv, 2-d-vi, 3-e-iii, 4-a-i, 5-b-v, 6-c-ii

65. Hidden Explosives

						*						
			C	O	R	V	O					
			T	E	N	E	R	I	F	E		
K	A	I	S	E	R	S	T	U	H	L		
				S	O	U	S	A	K	I		
F	U	E	R	T	E	V	E	N	T	U	R	A
				A	M	I	A	T	A			
					V	U	L	S	I	N	I	
			K	A	R	S						

Vesuvius in Italy; they are all active volcanoes of Europe.

66. When In Netherlands

1. Keukenhof Gardens
2. Leiden
3. Kinderdijk
4. Delta Works
5. Madurodam
6. Efteling
7. Apenheul
8. Anne Frank House

67. Park-ing Joys

1. Exmoor
2. Garajonay
3. Belovezhskaya
4. Cinque Terre
5. Hoge Veluwe
6. Bavarian Forest National Park
7. Pirin
8. Oulanka National Park
9. Durmitor
10. Cévennes.

68. Split Personalities

1. Roger Federer, Bjorn Borg
2. Sergey Bubka, Emil Zátopek
3. Cristiano Ronaldo, David Beckham
4. Michael Schumacher, Lewis Hamilton
5. Marianne Vos, Jeannie Longo
6. Nadia Comăneci, Svetlana Boginskaya
7. Annika Sörenstam, Anna Nordqvist
8. Alberto Tomba, Marcel Hirscher
9. Magnus Carlsen, Garry Kasparov
10. Carolina Kostner, Sonja Henie

69. Games of the Small States of Europe (GSSE)

1. Cyprus. But it had a population of less than 1 million when the group was formed in 1984.
2. Two
3. The Faroe Islands, but they have not been allowed because unlike the other participants the Faroes are neither a sovereign nation (they are an autonomous province of Denmark), nor are they a European Olympic Committee member.
4. City of San Marino, San Marino
5. 1985.
6. Reykjavik, Iceland.
7. Montenegro in 2009.

70. Political Statements

1. <u>Power</u> is like being a <u>lady</u>... if you have to tell people you are, you <u>aren't</u>.
2. You start giving out your hat, then you give your <u>coat</u>, then your shirt, then your <u>skin</u> and finally your <u>soul</u>.

3. Jesus was the first socialist, the first to seek a better life for mankind.
4. If you must break the law, do it to seize power: in all other cases observe it.
5. The world is weary of statesmen whom democracy has degraded into politicians.
6. For us democracy is a question of human dignity. And human dignity is political freedom.
7. When a truth is not given complete freedom, freedom is not complete.
8. To have another language is to possess a second soul.

71. Which Royal Am I?

1. Louis XVI
2. Leopold II
3. King Goerge V
4. Isabella II
5. Umberto I
6. Otto of Greece
7. Queen Maria II
8. Francis, who ruled as Francis II (as the last Holy Roman Emperor), and as Francis I (the first Emperor of Austria, which also included present-day Hungary)
9. Charles XIV John (as King of Sweden) and Charles III John (as King of Norway)
10. Christian IX
11. Nicholas I
12. Wilhelm II

72. Fashioning The Past

1. Wimple
2. Houppelande
3. Hennin
4. Farthingale
5. Jerkin
6. Aiglets
7. Jabot
8. Fichu
9. Panniers
10. Pantaloons
11. Girdle
12. Crinoline
13. Bloomers
14. Polonaise
15. Shirtwaist

73. Dancing Folk

M	A	Z	U	R	K	A	Z	S	T
H	I	A	K	L	O	P	E	G	B
A	D	N	K	P	L	Q	N	N	H
S	R	Y	U	S	O	U	O	I	D
A	R	O	H	E	L	E	L	G	I
P	J	O	T	A	T	O	O	G	L
I	U	A	S	T	R	A	P	O	I
K	Q	U	A	D	R	I	L	L	E
O	G	N	A	D	N	A	F	C	C
K	A	R	T	U	L	I	S	E	T

74. Bird IQ

Common Quail, Black Grouse, Little Bittern, Pygmy Cormorant, Spotted Crake, Whimbrel, Bluethroat, Grey Plover, Garganey, Yellow Wagtail, Fea's Petrel, Ruff, Mallard, Rock Ptarmigan, Sand martin, Eurasian jay.

QUICKBORN, GERMANY

75. Adieu! Adieu!

1. Adios
2. Au revoir
3. Arriverderci
4. La revedere
5. Auf weidersehen
6. Tot ziens
7. Adjo
8. Farvel
9. Ha det bra
10. Zegnaj